Light where we walk

Daily readings in Luke

Scripture Union

CONTENTS

Willie Black wrote the daily notes in *Light where we walk*. He seved as a Church of Scotland Minister in Kinlochbervie with Durness in NW Scotland for 12 years. The next 15 years were spent in Korea with OMF where he was mainly involved in helping pastors develop expository preaching. Having returned to Scotland, he has just been appointed to the High Church in Stornoway.

Neil Dougall prepared all the other material. He is minister of St David's Broomhouse Church in Edinburgh. He is married to Helen and they have two daughters. He loves cycling. His involvement with SU in Scotland began when he went to camp as a boy and has continued in various ways since then. At the moment he is a member of the Council and chairs the committee co-ordinating *Get Real!*.

Scripture Union Scotland
9 Canal Street
Glasgow
G4 0AB

ISBN 185999 2501

Publication prepared by Scripture Union England and Wales.
Cover design by Sue Jackson. Photo: Gary Cralle/The Image Bank

Editorial

Twenty years ago I was a senior pupil at school in Edinburgh. I had committed my life to Christ a few years earlier at a Scripture Union camp at Blairvaich and had just begun going to 'Open House', which was a get-together for senior pupils at the Edinburgh SU office. After one meeting I was chatting to Eleanor McIlroy, who was the Edinburgh SU worker at the time. Looking back, I guess this was one of the most significant conversations I've had in my life. Eleanor asked me if I was in the habit of reading the Bible and whether I used SU notes. I wasn't, so I said I'd tried it, but didn't feel it was for me. Of course that was just an excuse, and recognising it to be one, Eleanor encouraged me to really give it a shot. I went away and did, and it was then I began to establish a pattern of spending time each day with God, reading his word and praying.

In twenty years one thing hasn't changed: I still find the discipline of making time to be with God and read his Word, hard. The difference is, now I know it is for me. For looking back I can see that there has been a direct relationship between my spiritual progress and my commitment (or lack of it) to regular times with God.

I was very excited the first time I heard about *Get Real!* (SU Scotland's Gospel Project). Convinced from my own experience of the value of God's Word I am excited at the prospect of getting a gospel into the hands of Scottish young people. This is what changed my life; I long that it might change theirs. I therefore gladly accepted when I was asked to chair the committee which is coordinating *Get Real!*. At the first committee meeting, it was suggested, 'Why don't we produce a special set of Bible reading notes covering Luke's Gospel for our adult supporters?'

This seemed an excellent suggestion for two quite distinct reasons. First, it would be a way of involving the whole Scottish SU family in *Get Real!*. The main thrust is towards children and young people, but we don't want to ignore the supporters whose gifts have made *Get Real!* possible; and some of those adults will be in the front line, enabling the children and young people to interact with the Gospels. Second, it is a way in which we can address one of the most serious problems I believe the church is facing today: the dying habit of personal Bible reading.

Survey after survey reveals that people are no longer taking time regularly to pray and read their Bibles. Sales of Bible reading notes in Scotland suggest the SU family is not immune to this. Among school group leaders, prayer supporters, holiday team members, Council members and probably every other category you can think of, there are those who are trying to serve the Lord without being sustained by habits of personal devotion.

Of course I'm not suggesting there is anything magical about 'the Quiet Time'. That sort of legalism is damaging. Yet central to our faith is a relationship with the Father, through the Son and by the Spirit. The main way God has chosen to communicate with us is through his Word. It is as we allow God's Word to fill us, to grip us, to transform us, that we get to know him better and are energised to serve him. Without this we are at best anaemic Christians; at worst we burn out and give up. So I am deeply concerned that the absence of habits of personal devotion is robbing the church of men and women who are equipped and ready for the work God is calling us to.

In sending this book out with every copy of QSU, the coordinating committee is trying to do what Eleanor McIlroy did for me twenty years ago. She challenged me, 'Try it and see.' We challenge you, 'Use this book to try a pattern of regular Bible reading over the next three months.' Of course, Eleanor's challenge didn't remove all the difficulties I faced (and still struggle with). Simply issuing this book won't solve all the obstacles which prevent you establishing this habit. But my prayer is that you will taste and see, and in tasting discover the rich reward that comes from taking time to meet with God regularly. Then, three months from now, you won't just be continuing with the help of ongoing Bible reading notes (perhaps one of the SU ones mentioned in the colour pages), but will be encouraging others to do so too.

You may, however, be convinced about this already. In that case, why not give this book to someone you know with the challenge, 'Try regular Bible reading and see'!

Neil Dougall

Ways to use *Light where we walk*

1 Try the SU method of Bible reading, printed on the inside front cover.
The danger with any set of Bible reading notes is they can hinder what they are intended to help with. Instead of facilitating a meaningful meeting with God through his Word, they can become an end in itself. Reading the day's notes can actually become a substitute for communion with God. To help guard against this, the worldwide SU family has developed some simple steps. Many have found them a great help in ensuring their Bible reading is genuinely a meeting with God. Try these steps and see how you find them.

2 Let's journey together
Things we do together are easier to sustain than things we do on our own. Our Bible reading tends to be done on our own, and that's partly why we find it hard to stick at it. A simple solution is to begin to talk to each other about what we are reading and what God is saying to us through our meetings with him.

Light where we walk is a unique opportunity for the whole SU family in Scotland to journey together through the Bible. The notes are undated, but if we take the first note to be 1 April, then we can all start at the same time, even if some of us take a little longer to complete the journey.

Why not try at church (or at house groups or at SU meetings) taking a little time to share what you have been discovering through your reading of Luke's Gospel? While our Bible reading will still be personal, it will also become shared. This may be the sort of encouragement we need to make regular Bible reading part of our lives.

3 Pray for Get Real!
Suggestions for daily prayer are on the inside back cover.

Get Real!

Luke begins his Gospel by explaining: 'I made a careful study of everything and then decided to write and tell you exactly what took place. Honourable Theophilus, I have done this to let you know the truth about what you have heard' (Luke 1:3,4, CEV). The fundamental conviction behind *Get Real!* is that this same Gospel can do for young Scots what it did for Theophilus. Through reading it, they can discover the truth about Jesus. The vision of *Get Real!* is to encourage people into the Bible through Luke's Gospel, believing this will help them to meet Jesus and grow in faith.

To achieve this, a specially designed copy of Luke's Gospel has been produced in partnership with the National Bible Society of Scotland. It takes the form of a colour magazine, similar to those young people are used to buying in the newsagents. The CEV (Contemporary English Version), a recent translation, has been chosen because it is specifically intended to appeal to people who have little biblical background. Alongside the biblical text, icons have been placed to help readers understand it. For, sadly, the majority of young people in Scotland today have little exposure to the Bible; it is like a foreign book to them.

We have produced 125,000 Gospels. They will not simply be distributed to every schoolchild. Instead, they will be given in a setting which enables the young people to engage with what it says. So for example, they will be used in school SU groups and in Christian Focus Weeks, as part of camps and holiday clubs, and by churches in their ongoing work with young people. The whole SU family is being encouraged to think creatively and to organise special events which will enable young people to interact with Luke's Gospel and take away copies to read on their own.

It is anticipated there will be two main phases to *Get Real!*. During the Easter and summer holidays, camps and holiday clubs will focus on Luke. Then from August to December school SU groups will focus on Luke. Flexibility is, however, the key word. Far from requiring people to fit in with these phases, we are encouraging people to use *Get Real!*. whenever and however they can do so fruitfully. To assist in this, many supporting materials have been commissioned and produced.

Get involved in *Get Real!*

1 Prayer

Paul asks the Colossians, 'Pray for us, too, that God may open a door for our message, so that we may proclaim the mystery of Christ, for which I am in chains. Pray that I may proclaim it clearly, as I should' (Colossians 4:3,4).

Please pray that God would open hearts to the gospel, and that as it's explained it would be done so clearly. To help you, daily prayer points are listed on the inside back cover.

2 Use Get Real!

If you work with young people, could you make a special attempt sometime in 1998 to focus on Luke's Gospel? You can have the Gospels free of charge (while stocks last). All we ask is that you don't simply do a free distribution exercise, but prepare some kind of an activity which will encourage the young people to interact with the free Gospel you give them.

To help you with this, a range of materials has been commissioned and produced. The bulk of these are available at minimal cost. Materials are available for use in secondary and primary schools, for camps and holiday clubs, and for those working with primary children in Urban Priority Areas. A fuller list is printed in QSU, and more details, together with the Gospels, can be had from the SU office at Canal Street or from your local SU worker.

Why is reading the Bible important?

'Daily feeding on the Word of God seems to me to be indispensable to our Christian life, health and growth.'
John Stott

'Strong Christian discipleship depends on daily Bible reading. Much of today's weakness stems directly from neglecting Scripture.'
Michael Quicke

'A living encounter with the Bible makes all the difference in Christian life.'
Stephen Gaukroger

'The Bible is no mere library of religious literature. It is God's word of direction for how people should live in his world, his way.'
Cliver Calver

'Our postmodern world is in desperate need of Christians whose hearts and minds are fresh and clear from encountering God through Scripture. There really is no other way to grow.'
Jeff Lucas

'The Bible is one of God's vital "growth hormones". Without reading it and studying it regularly, as well as doing it, we simply cannot expect to grow.'
Derek J Tidball

Introduction to Luke

Author

Luke was not a Jew, but a Gentile. He was a well-educated man, a doctor by profession and one of Paul's travelling companions. He suddenly appears in Acts 16, where the text begins to talk about what 'we' did. From this people conclude that the author joined Paul at this point.

Luke's Gospel and the book of Acts are written by the same person, and go together. Luke's name never appears in either of them. However by working through the different friends Paul names in his letters, it seems certain that the author was Luke.

Theophilus

Luke wrote his books for an individual called Theophilus (Luke 1:3; Acts 1:1). It's unlikely that Theophilus was his real name; in Greek it simply means, 'Lover of God'. Luke calls him 'most excellent' which suggests he was an important person. He may have been a Roman Governor, or even a member of Caesar's household. To have publicly named this person might have been very dangerous for him, hence Luke's use of 'Lover of God'.

In today's language, Theophilus would have been described as a seeker. He had had some contact with the gospel and knew something about Jesus. Luke wrote to give him a full and proper account of Jesus' life and ministry, to enable Theophilus to 'know the certainty of the things he had been taught'.

What Luke's Gospel did for Theophilus, it has continued to do through the centuries and still does today. It introduces people to Jesus Christ and enables them to come to a reasoned and intelligent faith in him.

Luke's passion

There are great similarities between the Gospels of Matthew, Mark and Luke. Large sections of all three are almost identical. Each Gospel, however, has sections unique to it, which reveal the particular cares and concerns of each writer. The Holy Spirit's inspiration of the Gospel writers did not stamp a bland uniformity on their work; instead he used their distinct backgrounds and personalities to shape their writing.

In Luke's case we see a particular concern for people, and especially for the outsider. So, for example, when we look at the story of Jesus' birth in Matthew and Luke we discover different emphases. Matthew's prime concern is to show how Jesus' birth is the fulfilment of Old Testament scripture. Luke, in contrast, has a series of vivid stories about individuals. Beginning with Zechariah and ending with Simeon and Anna, Luke shows how ordinary people's lives were touched by the birth of Jesus.

Luke's experience as a doctor treating sick people makes his concern for individuals very natural. Equally, his experience as a non-Jew helps explain his concern for the outsider and the underprivileged. For in the society of Jesus day there was a very clear pecking order. Non-Jews, women and children were seen as having very little value. It wasn't just a case of first-class and second-class citizens, it was more that adult male Jews were citizens and everyone else wasn't.

There were more exclusions too. The poor tended to be given quite a hard time, and people who deliberately chose to break Jewish laws were also ostracised. All this meant there was a large circle of people on the fringes of society. Luke describes Jesus' care for these outsiders. He tells how Jesus raised a widow's son (7:11-17); of how the only leper who returned to thank Jesus was a foreigner (17:11-18); of Jesus seeking out Zacchaeus, an outcast because of his work as a tax collector (19:1-10); and of the news of Jesus' birth being entrusted to some extremely 'humble' shepherds (2:8-20).

The same pattern is repeated in the parables of Jesus found in Luke and not in the other Gospels. Their starring characters turned traditional roles on their head. For instead of prominent male Jews being the good guys, they appear as the bad ones. Think of the good Samaritan (10:26-37), the rich fool (12:13-21), the rich man and Lazarus (16:19-31), the persistent widow (18:1-8) and the Pharisee and the tax collector at prayer (18:9-14).

In Scotland today, many feel the church is not for them. They have the impression that the church is to do with respectable religion. People feel either that they don't want anything to do with this or, quite simply, that they are not good enough. Luke's Gospel, with its particular emphasis on Jesus' ministry to the outsider, is therefore especially relevant. It challenges those of us who are part of the church to be as active as Jesus was in reaching out to those on the fringes. It reassures those who feel excluded of Jesus' deep care for them and of his longing that they might experience his love.

Plan
Luke's aim is to show Jesus as the Saviour of the world. If one verse sums up the Gospel it's probably 19:10: 'The Son of Man came to seek and to save what was lost'.

Luke begins by describing Jesus' birth. 'Today in the town of David, a saviour has been born to you'. (2:11) Next, Luke presents Jesus' ministry in Galilee, culminating in Peter's declaration of faith (9:20). A key turning point is 9:51: 'Jesus resolutely set out for Jerusalem'. The next chapters relate Jesus' journey to Jerusalem, culminating in the Palm Sunday entry to that city (19:28-44). The last week of Jesus' life is described in detail, climaxing in

the crucifixion, when Jesus was still able to offer salvation to the penitent thief (23:42,43). The final chapter presents Jesus risen from the dead, strengthening his disciple's faith and ascending to heaven.

Outline

1:1-4
Introduction

1:5 - 2:52
Jesus comes into the world

3:1-20
John the Baptist prepares the way

3:21 - 4:12
Jesus' preparation: baptism and temptation

4:13 - 9:51
The Galilean ministry

9:51 - 19:27
On the road from Galilee to Jerusalem

19:28 - 23:56
The final week, centred on Jerusalem

24:1-53
Jesus, rising and ascending

Barren but blessed

There is not a circumstance which God cannot transform in a moment - trust him.

LUKE 1:1–7

Main verse: 'Both of them were upright in the sight of God, observing all the Lord's commandments and regulations blamelessly.'

Don't limit God (vs 1–4)

Luke was a very careful historian. Before he committed anything onto paper he carefully researched it to be sure of its authenticity. Initially, Luke wrote this Gospel to his friend, Theophilus, for instruction, but ultimately it was to strengthen the faith of all believers. There are two lessons we can learn here. First, we cannot limit God's divine work in us. Luke wrote specifically to one man, but God used his writing to benefit millions. God is not limited to the narrow confines of our plans. Second, yielding to God brings the best results. Luke is a good example of how God uses people, and of how God's wisdom and power are imparted to us. Do you believe that God can use you even in areas where you have no skills? In what area have you been called to serve him? Have you been faithful?

God is greater than your limitations (vs 5–7)

There are two lessons in these verses. The first is that our desired blessing is not automatically guaranteed in spite of our efforts to please God. Despite their faithful way of life, Zechariah and Elizabeth had no children. This reality refutes the theory which states that barrenness is a result of someone's sin. It is wise to examine our hearts for any form of sin when we face problems or disappointments. But it may well be that God has a greater purpose to be revealed in due time. Secondly, we see that God is in no way confined to the circumstances of our lives. God is greater than our circumstances. Elizabeth had been barren for years. She was old, but that didn't stop God from fulfilling his purpose in her life. Have you been trying to limit the work of God due to your lack of faith?

Prayer: Lord, allow me a greater vision to see your work which transcends human thought and circumstances.

Prepare the way for Jesus

Jesus still wants to come to the hearts of people.

LUKE 1:8–17

Main verse: 'And he will go before the Lord, in the spirit and power of Elijah, to turn the hearts of the fathers to their children and the disobedient to the wisdom of the righteous – to make ready a people prepared for the Lord.'

God answers prayer (vs 8–13)

God surprises us unexpectedly. Zechariah and Elizabeth had no doubt regularly and consistently prayed for a son. And when they least expected it, God answered their prayer. This child would be no ordinary son; and so God brought special circumstances to announce his birth. Zechariah received a chance to go into the holiest place in the temple. What seemed like a chance was, in fact, God's divine plan. God sent one of his special angels to announce the birth to Zechariah. God indeed fulfilled his promise to Zechariah and Elizabeth, who persevered in prayer. Have you given up praying for something because God has not seemed to answer? Why not persevere in your praying?

God prepares his people (vs 14–17)

John the Baptist was entrusted with the special task of preparing people's hearts for Jesus' coming. John's unique task must, in a way, be repeated in each of our lives. We need to prepare the way for Jesus to come into the lives of those who don't know him. To be really useful for God, we need to be separate from the things of the world, willing to be different for God. We need to be Spirit-filled and dependent on his power. Most of all, we need to point people to Jesus. Are you prepared to speak out against sin and rebellion? There can be no greater joy than being used of God to bring someone to Christ. Do people see Christ's truth through your lifestyle? Are you leading others to Jesus?

Prayer: Almighty God, make me a useful instrument that I may direct others to you.

God cares for you

God is concerned about the most personal problems of our lives.

LUKE 1:18–25

Main verse: '"The Lord has done this for me," she said, "In these days he has shown his favour and taken away my disgrace among the people."'

God gives a sign (vs 18–22)

Zechariah found it difficult to believe what the angel was saying to him (v 18). It must disappoint God when we express unbelief in what God is able to do. So often we make the mistake that Zechariah made by focusing on the circumstances of our lives rather than fixing our minds on the character of God. Zechariah knew that God had worked in similar circumstances in the past but still he found it difficult to believe God's promise. God was very patient with Zechariah and accepted his request for a sign. But for his unbelief, Zechariah was not able to speak for a given time and his unbelief was exposed before the people. Are you willing to put your trust in the Word of God, or are you always looking for other signs?

God shows favour (vs 23–25)

For Elizabeth, her child was evidence of God's favour and grace to her. She was not primarily concerned about her son's role in history. This child was evidence that God was interested in her and in her personal concern at being a disgrace for being childless. She realised in the most special way that God was able to remove her disgrace. Simultaneously, God fulfilled his prophecies of old and his plan for his people, and became personally involved in the details of one woman's life. This is the God we worship – in control of history and yet concerned about each human being. In what way has God shown interest in your problems? Will you give thanks right now for the Lord's favour upon you?

Prayer: Lord, thank you that you are willing to be personally and intricately involved in my life.

Nothing is impossible to God

There is nothing God cannot do through the life of a willing servant.

LUKE 1:26–38

Main verse: 'The angel answered, "The Holy Spirit will come upon you, and the power of the Most High will overshadow you. So the holy one to be born will be called the Son of God."'

A fearful servant (vs 26–31)
When God needed someone to bear his Son, he did not choose a woman of high status. Rather, in an obscure and despised village of Nazareth, he found a young girl who was engaged to be married. There are elements of surprise and fear when God expresses his desire to use us in his service. Mary was no exception. What God was asking of her was costly. It could cost her relationship with Joseph. It could cost her reputation. But, as costly as it was, there was great blessing to follow, because she was called to bear the Son of God. When God calls us to some task for him, we need to count the cost and yet consider the blessing that comes from obedience. What costly task is God giving you today?

A willing servant (vs 32–38)
The angel encourages Mary to commit herself in obedience to God. First of all, he reminds her of the great privilege of obedience. The One she bears will be the Son of God who will reign for ever (v 33). Next, he explains to her very simply how the Holy Spirit will come upon her (v 35). Thirdly, in order to confirm God's power, he tells her that Elizabeth, even in her old age, will bear a son. Finally, he reminds her that nothing is impossible for God (v 37). Having carefully considered this message, the fearful servant is transformed into a willing servant. With a willing, obedient servant and the power of the Holy Spirit there is no limit to what God can accomplish. Have you agreed to be used of God in any way he calls you to be? Will you be the obedient servant he needs today?

Prayer: Lord, I choose to obey you in the matters that you bring to my life this day.

The blessings of belief

Do you leap for joy at the name of Jesus?

LUKE 1:39–45

Main verse: 'Blessed is she who has believed that what the Lord has said to her will be accomplished!'

Filled with the Spirit
(vs 39–41)

Mary couldn't wait to go and see her cousin Elizabeth. Perhaps she wanted to confirm for herself the news of Elizabeth's baby and also share her good news. Perhaps she just needed to have fellowship with someone who was obviously involved with her in the great plan of God. It is reassuring and renewing to have fellowship with people who share common visions. Elizabeth and Mary both experienced wonderful events. There were two immediate results of the faith of these women. First, there was joy as the baby leapt in Elizabeth's womb. John the Baptist knew exactly who Jesus was and expressed his joy even before they were both born. Belief in God always results in joy. Second, Elizabeth was filled with the Holy Spirit. God had promised that her son would be filled with the Holy Spirit from birth. Are you filled with the Holy Spirit? How does being Spirit-filled make a difference in your life?

Blessed beyond belief
(vs 42–45)

When we are obedient to God, we become a channel of blessing to others. Elizabeth was blessed much by Mary's presence. She felt honoured that the mother of the Son of God came to her house. Blessing is never meant to be kept to ourselves but to be shared with others, which is exactly what Elizabeth did. Elizabeth also understood that blessing is not based on what we *do* but rather on what we *believe*. It is when we trust God's Word that we will really come into a blessed life. We don't need to strive after blessings, we just need to believe in the Word of God and receive it. What kind of blessing will you share with others today?

Prayer: Lord of truth, help me to believe in your Word that I may be a blessing to others today.

Rejoice in God your Saviour

Even in the midst of fulfilling his great plan for history,
God attends to your concern.

LUKE 1:46–56

Main verses: 'And Mary said, "My soul glorifies the Lord and my spirit rejoices in God my Saviour."'

God cares for you (vs 46–49)

Mary realised that God had a specific plan and purpose for her life. She rejoiced in the mighty God who had done something special for her. It is obvious from her words that she didn't feel she deserved the honour God was giving her. Perhaps we can learn from Mary. If we want to be used for God's service, what kind of person do we need to become? We need to have a repentant heart. Even Mary needed a Saviour; she was not sinless. We need to admit our sin before God, and acknowledge God as our Lord. Remember that we are his servants, and must humbly be willing to obey him in everything. Being called by God is the most wonderful privilege. What specific plan does God have for you? Do you count it a privilege to serve the Lord?

God is involved in history (vs 50–56)

While Mary could not get over the fact that God was concerned about her and had a plan for her life, she also realised that God had a grander plan for all of history. God is concerned about politics and about those who have power to rule over others. If God decides, he can change a ruler at his will. God is concerned about problems of justice in society, and therefore will deal with those who misuse their riches and power. God is concerned about the problem of hunger in our world, and is able to restore the world's natural resources which people have abused. But most of all, God is concerned with his own people. Don't forget that in Jesus Christ, you have become one of the true descendants of Abraham, and therefore come under God's sovereign care. How is your perspective of God? Do you limit God's concerns for this world?

Prayer: Lord, thank you for caring for me even as you are mindful of the concerns of this world.

The birth of John the Baptist

God responds to our obedience by giving abundant blessing.

LUKE 1:57–66

Main verse: 'Everyone who heard this wondered about it, asking, "What then is this child going to be?" For the Lord's hand was with him.'

The importance of obedience (vs 57–61)

In due course, Elizabeth gave birth to a son, which brought much rejoicing before God. The birth of John the Baptist was an expression of God's mercy and grace. All that we will ever have and receive is a direct result of God's grace; but having received God's grace, we must be careful not to lose it by our disobedience. Elizabeth and Zechariah were determined not to make that mistake. They were careful to keep the law of God, and had John circumcised on the eighth day after his birth. They were also obedient in naming the child 'John' as God had commanded (v 60). It was against their tradition of naming him after a relative, but they followed God's command. Blessings can be lost when we prefer to keep our traditions rather than obey God. What traditions have caused conflict in your obedience to God?

The blessings of obedience (vs 62–66)

Obedience is not the source of blessing – God's grace is. But our obedience is the means of releasing that blessing. The moment Zechariah wrote the name of John on a writing tablet, in obedience to God's command, he was healed of his inability to speak and began praising God. His life was filled with a sense of joy and privilege at what God had done. People who were there realised that they were witnessing an extraordinary plan of God. The blessings God offers to his servant often spill over into the hearts of others. Most importantly, these people caught a glimpse of hope that God was again at work among his people. What blessings can you rejoice in today? How does Zechariah's simple obedience encourage you?

Prayer: Lord, thank you for all the blessings you have given me.

Prepare the way for him

God graciously prepares the hearts of people to receive Jesus.

LUKE 1:67–80

Main verse: 'Praise be to the Lord, the God of Israel, because he has come and has redeemed his people.'

God saves his people (vs 67–75)

Filled with the Holy Spirit, Zechariah prophesied about the coming of Jesus. As far as he was concerned it had already taken place. Hearing about Jesus Christ was sufficient for Zechariah to believe that God had already accomplished the salvation of his people. God's Word never fails; he will keep his promise. If God makes a covenant with his people, you can count on his faithfulness. Zechariah believed that Jesus would save us from our enemies – from Satan and sin (v 71). Zechariah also believed that Jesus would save us for a special purpose – he would save us so that we could serve God in holiness and righteousness without fear (v 74). Do you believe God always keeps his Word? Have you been set free from your enemies?

Prepare others for salvation (vs 76–80)

God is aware of the hardened hearts of his people. So before he offers salvation through Jesus Christ, he softens the hearts of people. He did this through the ministry of John the Baptist. These days he does so by the ministry of the Holy Spirit. If people are going to receive salvation, they need to be informed about Jesus – about who he is and what he can do. They must be conscious of their sin and through repentance receive forgiveness. They must realise that their salvation depends solely on the mercy and grace of God and not on anything they do. They must come to Jesus who alone grants peace. The ministry of John the Baptist served to lead people to Christ. Who are you praying for these days so that they can come to Jesus? Have you put your trust in the work of the Holy Spirit, or are you relying on your own effort?

Prayer: Lord God, I am eternally grateful for being saved. Use me to reach others with the message of salvation.

The birth of Jesus

Jesus came to be with us in our world.

LUKE 2:1–7

Main verse: 'And she gave birth to her firstborn, a son. She wrapped him in cloths and placed him in a manger, because there was no room for them in the inn.'

Jesus – born into history (vs 1–5)

Out of all the Gospel writers, Luke was most concerned with historical facts. He placed Jesus firmly in a historical setting. Jesus was not a myth. He was a man born into this world at a specific time and place in history. He was a real man. All the events which happened in Jesus' life were real. It was necessary, if the scriptures were to be fulfilled, that Jesus be born in Bethlehem and not in Nazareth where his mother was living (v 4). God arranged for the Roman government to call for a census which would guarantee Mary's presence in Bethlehem at the right time. God is in control of human history. God is in control of our circumstances. How have you witnessed that God is in control of your life these days?

Jesus – born into our world (vs 6,7)

The actual place of Jesus' birth has so much to teach us. He was born in a stable and was laid in a manger. There was no room for him in the inn. We clearly learn that Jesus came into this world to be with us. He came to share in our most difficult circumstances; he came to share in our poverty; he came to be with us in our rejection – he came to be with us in our homelessness. Because Jesus shared with us in all aspects of our lives, we know that he is able to understand and can empathise with us in every problem. There is no problem beyond Jesus' power. By becoming a man, he touched the lowest places in our world. Are you aware that God is really with you in your problems? Does it comfort you to know that Jesus has shared in your suffering and pain?

Prayer: Jesus, I trust you as my faithful friend, sharing my joys as well as my sorrows. Keep me close to you always.

Good news!

The good news of Jesus is news that everyone needs to hear.

LUKE 2:8–20

Main verse: 'But the angel said to them, "Do not be afraid. I bring you good news of great joy that will be for all the people."'

News worth hearing (vs 8–14)

Interestingly, God announced his Son's birth to ordinary people engaged in their work. The angels proclaimed to the shepherds that the news of Jesus was for all men. It is still true today. The good news of Jesus Christ is for everyone. First of all, this good news deals with fear. The very first words of the angel were, 'Don't be afraid.' The gospel of Jesus Christ is able to take away our fears. Secondly, the gospel is news of joy. It is a gospel that brings real joy to people of all circumstances. Thirdly, it is news of salvation. Jesus had come specifically to save people from their sin and from judgement. This news was certainly worth hearing. Is your life full of joy? Is it full of fear?

News worth declaring (vs 15–20)

When the shepherds went and saw Jesus, they informed Mary of what the angels had said to them. It brought comfort to Mary and she treasured those words in her heart to help her through difficult times in the future (v 19). As soon as the shepherds left the place, they told others about the child and about their experience. It was news worth telling. It was news which everyone needed to hear. How selfish it would have been if they had kept it to themselves. They realised that such news revealed God's grace and rejoiced in declaring it. Do you think the news of Jesus is worth declaring to others? Do you praise God every day for this good news? Is there a particular person you need to share with today?

Prayer: Lord, I am grateful for the good news of Jesus. Help me to be prayerful and diligent in declaring it to others.

How can you please God?

God desires obedience to the leading of the Holy Spirit.

LUKE 2:21–35

Main verses: 'For my eyes have seen your salvation … a light for revelation to the Gentiles and for glory to your people Israel.'

Be obedient to the law (vs 21–24)

In today's passage, two important principles are illustrated. First, by Mary and Joseph's example, we see the need to be obedient to God's law. They were careful to keep the law by having Jesus circumcised on the eighth day and by making the required offering for him. These things were necessary so he could die in our place on the cross. He had to be recognised as one who kept the law perfectly so that he could save us from it. Certainly, keeping the law is not a prerequisite for our salvation; however, having been saved we do not disregard the law. How do you see your life in light of God's law?

Be led by the Spirit (vs 25–35)

The second important principle is illustrated for us in the life of Simeon. He was a man who was sensitive to the leading of the Holy Spirit (vs 25,26). He was filled with the Spirit. As a result, he was at the right place at the right time to meet the Lord Jesus according to God's promise. God used Simeon to declare Jesus' identity and mission to Joseph and Mary. Jesus would bring hope to both Jews and Gentiles. He would be a blessing to many but at the same time would bring conflict to others. God is looking for people like Mary and Joseph who were obedient to his Word. God uses people like Simeon who are filled with and led by the Holy Spirit. Are you filled with the Spirit? How is it manifested?

Prayer: Father, I rely on the Holy Spirit to lead a triumphant life, a life in obedience to your Word.

What are your priorities?

Our relationship to God based on his Word is the top priority in life.

LUKE 2:36–40

Main verse: 'And the child grew and became strong; he was filled with wisdom, and the grace of God was upon him.'

Live close to God (vs 36–38)
Once more we see that people who live their lives close to God are used of God as a blessing to others. Anna did not allow the death of her husband to distance her from God. On the contrary, she seized the opportunity in her singleness to dedicate her life to God. She chose to live in the temple, close to the presence of God. She prayed and fasted often, and her commitment to God bore many fruits in her life. She was a prophetess and an encourager of others who were seeking more blessing from God. She had an opportunity to meet Jesus. How much time do you give to God? How will you live close to the Lord today?

Be obedient to his Word (vs 39,40)
Again, it is emphasised how Mary and Joseph were obedient to the Word of God. They returned home only after they completed what was demanded by the law. Luke doesn't tell us, but that could only take place after they had gone to Egypt (Matthew 2). Having parents who were committed to pleasing God, Jesus had the ideal environment for his growth. In an environment full of God's grace and wisdom, we cannot doubt that Jesus grew into the kind of person God wanted him to be. If you are a parent, what kind of environment do you provide for your children? Although Jesus may have lacked many material things available in his day, he had the best spiritual resources available for him. Do you and your spouse faithfully obey the Lord? Have you witnessed the effect your obedience has on your children and others around you?

Prayer: Lord, instruct me to realise the most important things in life and to focus on them without wavering. Fill me with your wisdom and grace.

Do you know who you are?

Do you know God's purpose for your life?

LUKE 2:41-52

Main verse: '"Why were you searching for me?" he asked. "Didn't you know I had to be in my Father's house?"'

Jesus learns who he is (vs 41–47)

It may be Jesus' first visit to Jerusalem to keep the Passover. Of all the Jewish feasts, the Passover best symbolised Jesus' mission. This must have been a poignant and perhaps testing time for him as he began to consider the very purpose for which he had come. No doubt the consciousness of his identity had begun to dawn on him, as he considered who he was and what he had come to accomplish. Part of the cost Jesus paid to become a human being was that he had to grow like everyone else. His penetrating questions astonished those who were listening to him. How enthusiastic are you to learn more about the things of God? Have you taken time to seek and know what God wants of you?

Jesus continues to grow (vs 48–52)

Jesus' parents had much to learn. All parents must accept that there does come a time when they must allow their children to become independent men and women. Mary and Joseph have just begun to learn this lesson. There is one relationship which must take priority even over the natural relationship of parents and children and that is our relationship with God. Jesus realised that his ultimate responsibility was to God, his Father in heaven. Yet he submitted himself to his earthly parents and returned home with them. To grow spiritually we must submit to God and his Word. Is your heart in full submission to God? Do you obey his Word?

Prayer: Dear Father, guide me to find the specific purpose you have for my life and to follow it at all costs.

Prepare the way for the Lord

How can you help people come to faith in Jesus?

LUKE 3:1–6

Main verse: 'He went into all the country around the Jordan, preaching a baptism of repentance for the forgiveness of sins.'

Preach the gospel (vs 1–3)

Luke emphasised historical facts to give the gospel authenticity. God works in and through the lives of specific men and women. Here, God was working through the life and ministry of John the Baptist. God's way does not always conform to our expectations. Naturally we would expect God to work through the high priests of that day, but God bypassed them to use his servant John. We must not limit God's choice of people. Also, we learn that God works in his own time, in his own way. At the appropriate time, God called John the Baptist to begin his ministry of preaching the gospel. How faithful are you in preaching the gospel? Do you tell others of the need for repentance?

Prepare the way for Jesus (vs 4–6)

Luke taught that nothing happens in history by accident. Because God is sovereign, he has everything planned. Long ago he prophesied the coming of John the Baptist, and now that word has been fulfilled. God always fulfils his Word. The Word is clear that only Jesus can save men and women from their sin. Not even John the Baptist could save anyone. The best that John the Baptist, or anyone else, can do is to prepare the way for Jesus to come into the lives of men and women. Are there any obstacles in your life which may block the way to others' putting their faith in Christ? Can you pray for a changed life so that others will see a reason to believe in Jesus?

Prayer: Lord, remove any obstacles in my life that might cause others to stumble while seeking you. Please bless others through my life in Christ.

Repent!

Repentance without real fruit is not true repentance.

LUKE 3:7-14

Main verse: 'Produce fruit in keeping with repentance. And do not begin to say to yourselves, "We have Abraham as our father." For I tell you that out of these stones God can raise up children for Abraham.'

Repent of your sin (vs 7–9)

John the Baptist exposed two particular problems existing in the lives of the Jews. First of all, they failed to see the need for repentance. They thought that they were spiritually secure because they were descendants of Abraham (v 8). They thought that being Jewish automatically meant having security with God. John shattered that illusion when he told them that God is able to raise up Abraham's children from stones. The one thing that guarantees a secure relationship with God is forgiveness of sin by faith in Christ. Secondly, when the Jews acknowledged the need for repentance, they were content with a token repentance by word only. John makes it clear that repentance without fruit is meaningless (v 8).

Bear fruits of repentance (vs 10–14)

Real repentance results in changed behaviour. What kind of changes did John expect to see as a result of repentance? He expected people to be more kind and considerate (v 11). He expected them to be free from their love of material possessions and to willingly share what they had (vs 11-13). People were to be honest in all that they did, not to lie and cheat (v 14). He expected people not to abuse their authority or position for their own advantage, but wanted people to learn contentment in any situation. John expected people to repent in action as well as in words. Do you see these fruits of real repentance in your life?

Prayer: Lord, search my heart that I may truly repent of my sins. May my repentance prove true in the fruit I bear.

Jesus and the Holy Spirit

Jesus will baptise you with the Holy Spirit.

LUKE 3:15-22

Main verse: 'John answered them all, "I baptise you with water. But one more powerful than I will come, the thongs of whose sandals I am not worthy to untie. He will baptise you with the Holy Spirit and with fire."'

Jesus – the baptiser with the Holy Spirit (vs 15–18)

Many people thought John the Baptist was the long-expected Messiah. John was quick to deny such assumptions. He refused to receive the glory that belonged to Christ, and he emphasised the unique power of Jesus Christ (v 16). He confessed his own unworthiness before the purity and holiness of Jesus. He emphasised the symbolic nature of his own baptism as well as the baptism of the Holy Spirit and power which Jesus himself would give. We cannot be filled by the Holy Spirit apart from Jesus. We cannot experience a Spirit-filled life if we do not allow Jesus to cleanse us from our sins. Are you filled with the Spirit and his power? What can you learn from the example of John the Baptist?

Jesus – baptised in the Holy Spirit (vs 19–22)

Some kind of suffering is inevitable for those who are faithful to God's calling. John was imprisoned and eventually executed for his faithfulness to God. Jesus would suffer greatly for his faithfulness to the Father, but he was fully equipped for his ministry. Jesus never asks us to do anything which he was not prepared to do himself. Thus, he submitted to the baptism of repentance like others. He was sinless but willingly became like a sinner for us. He had power over heaven and earth, but he became as one with no power. He was the eternal Son of God, but humbled himself to become one of us for our benefit. Jesus humbled himself for you; will you humble yourself to him today?

Prayer: Father God, fill me with your Holy Spirit so I may proclaim your majestic power.

Jesus: son of man, Son of God

Jesus was fully divine and fully human at the same time.

LUKE 3:23-38

Main verse: 'The son of Enosh, the son of Seth, the son of Adam, the son of God.'

Jesus – the man of God (vs 23–29)

Luke draws our attention to three truths. First, Jesus was a man. Luke would not have bothered to trace the human ancestry of Jesus Christ if he did not believe this fact. He established Jesus' concrete identity in history – in our world. Second, he suggests that Jesus was more than just a man. Joseph was his legal father, but he was not his true father. His true father was God in heaven. Jesus was fully God and fully man. Third, Luke tells us that Jesus came for a specific purpose. When he was thirty years old, Jesus began his ministry. In those days a man was thought to be fully mature by the time he was thirty, which was when priests began to serve God in that capacity. The priestly work of Christ is implied here. Do you believe that Jesus is God who came as a man for your sake?

Jesus – the second Adam (vs 30–38)

Luke's genealogy of Christ traces back to Adam and ultimately to God himself. It is significant to note that we are unfamiliar with many names on this list. you don't need to be famous to be used by God. Many of these people weren't famous, yet each person had a significant place in the line of Jesus. There are also some well-known names on this list. God had promised that Jesus would come from the line of David and Judah, and that through Abraham the whole world would be blessed. God is faithful to his promises. Adam was God's first creation. Tragically, he failed to meet God's plan. Now Jesus came as the second Adam and fulfilled God's great mission. Do you believe that God can really use you? Will you affirm your faith that Jesus has accomplished everything for you?

Prayer: Lord, thank you that Jesus accomplished what could not be done by me: the gift of eternal salvation for believers.

Jesus – tempted by the devil

What is the best way to overcome temptation?

LUKE 4:1–13

Main verses: 'Jesus, full of the Holy Spirit, returned from the Jordan and was led by the Spirit in the desert, where for forty days he was tempted by the devil.'

Be filled with the Spirit (vs 1–4)

When Jesus was baptised and was preparing to begin his ministry, the devil came and tempted him. When we are committed to love and serve God, the devil is more likely to tempt us. He robs us of blessings we have received and discourages us at the start of a new work for God. Ironically, it was the Spirit who led Jesus into the desert. God allows temptations to come our way but will always provide a way of escape (1 Corinthians 10:13). The Holy Spirit enables us to overcome temptations through dependence on God's Word. Often Satan tempts us by manipulating our present weakness and causing us to doubt who we are in Christ. Remember that you are a child of God. If you are full of the Spirit, have you anything to fear?

Use the sword of the Spirit (vs 5–13)

Each time Jesus was tempted by the devil, he rebuffed that temptation by quoting specific verses from the Bible. He used the sword of the Spirit – that is, the Word of God – because he knew that the devil had no answer to God's truth. To have the same kind of defence, we need to know our Bible thoroughly. We need to develop a discipline of memorising Scripture verses. However, keep in mind that Satan also knows the Bible; and while he hates its truth, he will use it perversely to trap us. What Satan really wants through temptation is to win our allegiance. Be on guard, because Satan is waiting for that right moment to trap us. Is overcoming temptation important enough that you will commit yourself to knowing God's Word? Do you trust the Word of God as the 'sword of the Spirit'?

Prayer: Lord, equip me by your Spirit and your Word to be victorious over Satan.

Jesus – filled with the Spirit

It is difficult to live out our obedience to Christ before those who know us closely.

LUKE 4:14–30

Main verse: 'The Spirit of the Lord is on me, because he has anointed me to preach good news to the poor ... to proclaim freedom for the prisoners and recovery of sight for the blind, to release the oppressed.'

Jesus speaks with authority (vs 14–21)

Jesus was now ready to begin his ministry, filled with the power of the Holy Spirit. One of the first places he went to proclaim God's Word was his own town of Nazareth (v 16). It is very difficult to witness to those who are closest to us, who know us best (v 24). On his weekly visit to a synagogue, Jesus seized the opportunity to read the Scriptures. He chose a passage which summed up his ministry on earth, a passage which revealed that he was the Messiah sent by God. Are you prepared to speak out clearly in witness of what God has done for you? Our testimony must be based on the Word of God. Do the people in your home see you as a faithful follower of Christ?

Jesus exposes hypocrisy (vs 22–30)

At first, the people in Nazareth were delighted by what they saw in Jesus. No doubt they wanted to bask in the glory and praise which Jesus was receiving wherever he went. But Jesus is always able to see behind our words into our hearts. Jesus could see the hypocrisy in the hearts of these people. There was no real commitment to Jesus in their hearts. They were not prepared to admit that he was who he said he was; they were not ready to submit to him. In fact, they tried to kill him. They learned, however, that Jesus' authority was not confined to his words only and that, in fact, no one could harm him until it was God's time. How is your commitment to Jesus – is it one of words only, or have you a heart truly devoted to him?

Prayer: Mighty Lord, encourage me to witness boldly and to live out an authentic Christian life before my family and friends.

The authority of Jesus

Jesus has power and authority to deal with all forms of evil.

LUKE 4:31-37

Main verse: 'All the people were amazed and said to each other, "What is this teaching? With authority and power he gives orders to evil spirits and they come out!"'

Jesus teaches with authority (vs 31,32)

Jesus taught with authority because of who he was. People were amazed to see him teaching with real authority (v 32). His Word delivered power to touch lives and to change circumstances. Jesus taught with authority because he was filled with the Spirit. Today, people called by God to preach his Word can teach with the same authority when they are filled with the Spirit. Jesus taught with authority because he based his teaching on the Word of God. Teachings based on human knowledge and opinions cannot claim this kind of authority – only God's Word gives real authority to our teaching. Do you always base your teaching on the Word of God? Are you convinced that the message people must hear is God's Word more than your personal views?

Jesus has power over evil spirits (vs 33–37)

Jesus' authority was not limited to his teaching, but he had come to deal with the basic problem of evil. We learn that evil spirits know exactly who Jesus is – they recognise him as the Holy One of God (v 34). Though they are aware that his power is much greater than theirs, they refuse to surrender and submit to the Lord. We also see that evil spirits try to confuse people. Jesus silences the demons quickly because he didn't want people to be confused by their words. Finally, we see how Jesus' Word alone is powerful to deal with evil as these spirits succumb to Jesus' commands. Are you ever afraid of evil spirits? Do these passages help and encourage you to trust Jesus and his Word?

Prayer: Lord, I stand in awe before your mighty power. Strengthen me to stand firm against the evil one.

All need to hear the gospel

Jesus' top priority was to preach the gospel to all people.

LUKE 4: 38–44

Main verse: 'But he said, "I must preach the good news of the kingdom of God to the other towns also, because that is why I was sent."'

Jesus deals with sickness (vs 38–41)

Jesus' love led him to minister to those who were sick. When Peter's mother-in-law was sick, Jesus responded to his disciple's request to heal her (vs 38,39). There are two simple lessons here for us. First of all, our lack of understanding in regard to healing shouldn't restrict us from seeking Jesus' power. God invites us to lift up our troubles to him in prayer. Secondly, we should not limit Jesus' work to one particular method. Here, he heals first by rebuking the illness. Did Jesus detect that this illness was caused directly by the influence of evil spirits? Next, we see him healing many people by laying hands on them. How do you understand the way Jesus heals today? Is there someone you should be praying for?

Jesus preaches the gospel (vs 42–44)

People wanted to keep Jesus in their town because he met their desperate needs. It must have been tempting for Jesus to stay in a comfortable setting, but he refused mere comfort and the tendency to focus his ministry on the sensational or on temporary solutions to problems. That was not why he had come into the world. The focus of his ministry had to be on the eternal – on the salvation of human souls. Jesus was willing to help people with their physical problems, but his main ministry was to proclaim the gospel to a multitude of people. Jesus had to keep his priorities in order. Have you got your priorities in order? How is your perspective – do you focus on the eternal or on the temporary things of the world?

Prayer: Lord, grant me a compassionate heart that prays for all people to hear the gospel.

Fishers of men

Jesus has a special plan for your life.

LUKE 5:1-11

Main verse: 'Don't be afraid; from now on you will catch men.'

Don't rely on your experience (vs 1–5)

Experience is something God can really use when we submit ourselves to him. Peter was an experienced fisherman. Unfortunately, the more experienced people become, the more knowledgeable they think they are. They are tempted to rely on their own experience without God. Our experiences can easily become a barrier in our relationship with God. Peter was no exception. He was quick to depend on his experience rather than Jesus; but he decided to obey Jesus' request to cast the nets. Even though God may surprise us with the things he asks us to do, we must obey him. Have you ever found yourself thinking that you know better than God? Are you relying on your own experience or on God?

Trust Jesus (vs 6–11)

Our expertise in one area does not necessarily restrict us from being instruments of God in other areas. Because God desires his people to trust him, he may call us to unfamiliar tasks. Jesus called these fishermen to become fishers of men. By the unusually large catch of fish, they learned to trust Jesus (vs 8,9). He knows best and desires to provide for his followers. He is not afraid to expose sin or pride in our lives in order to bring us closer to God. He wants us to be willing to leave everything and follow him. The most humble people were greatly used by God. Is God calling you to do something different for him? Will you trust him?

Prayer: Lord, forgive me of my arrogant reliance on my gifts and experience. Help me trust in you alone.

Willing and obedient

Jesus is always willing to meet your need.

LUKE 5:12-16

Main verse: 'Jesus reached out his hand and touched the man. "I am willing," he said. "Be clean!" And immediately the leprosy left him.'

Jesus is willing (vs 12,13)

Leprosy sufferers experienced so much rejection in their lives that it is hardly surprising that this man was worried whether Jesus would be willing to heal him or not. He did not doubt the power of Jesus to heal him, but he did doubt his willingness. There are many mysteries in the realm of Christian healing. We cannot understand exactly why Jesus in some cases refused to heal those who asked him. Nevertheless we are sure that he does have the power to heal when it is his will to do so. Here, Jesus dispelled the leprosy sufferer's worries by his willingness to hear him and by daring to touch him. Are you ever tempted to think that you are too unworthy for Jesus to help? He is willing. He is able.

Jesus is obedient (vs 14–16)

Jesus was obedient to the law of God. Lepers had to go to a priest and be declared clean by him. Jesus instructed the man to submit to this law. Jesus' obedience to God encompasses a higher purpose. Jesus did not come simply to heal the sick. He came to die on the cross for sinners. With popularity for his healing power, there were temptations for him to be diverted from the real task he had come to accomplish (v 15). Jesus often told those he healed not to disclose such miracles (v 14). And often he went away to be alone with God in order to keep his mind focused on his ultimate mission (v 16). Are you fulfilling the task God wants you to do, or are you working towards what will bring you the most glory?

Prayer: Lord, thank you for being involved in my life, to bestow healing and strength. Lead me to the path of obedience.

Receive forgiveness now

Jesus has the authority to forgive your sins.

LUKE 5:17–26

Main verse: '"But that you may know that the Son of Man has authority on earth to forgive sins...." He said to the paralysed man, "I tell you, get up, take your mat and go home."'

Power to heal (vs 17–20)
The power which Jesus had to heal the sick was in fact God's power. It seems that sometimes that power was more readily available than at other times. Does that help us understand why sometimes people are healed and sometimes they are not when we pray? Also, in this case there are other important elements in his healing. The man's friends showed remarkable perseverance and ingenuity. They were not willing to give up until their friend met Jesus. Are some people not healed because they give up too easily? We notice that Jesus was impressed by their faith which made their friend's healing possible. And in this case the problem was not purely physical. There existed a connection between the man's sin and his sickness. Forgiveness had to come first.

Power to forgive (vs 21–26)
Jesus' primary purpose in coming to us was to deal with the problem of sin, not our physical problems. Though he was willing to help our physical ailments, his supreme mission was to deal with our sins. When Jesus claimed to have the power to forgive sins, he was, in fact, claiming to be God, for only God has the power to forgive sins (vs 21,24). Naturally, the Pharisees were appalled at his claim. Jesus clearly demonstrated that he had this power by healing the paralysed man. There is no need to wait; we can receive that forgiveness right now. Do you need to repent and confess any sins to him right now? Will you recognise Jesus as your Lord by receiving his forgiveness?

Prayer: Lord, cleanse me of any iniquities which hinder your work. Make me whole by healing the pains in my life.

New wine needs new skins

A new heart can be filled with the Holy Spirit.

LUKE 5:27–39

Main verse: 'And no one pours new wine into old wineskins. If he does, the new wine will burst the skins, the wine will run out and the wineskins will be ruined.'

Jesus makes people new (vs 27–35)

Jesus called the most unlikely people to be his disciples. For instance, he called a tax collector – one of the lowest and most despised people of his day. Why did Jesus do that? Why didn't Jesus select from among the religious leaders? Jesus explained that he called those who were aware of their sin and their need of his help. Many religious leaders assumed they were self-righteous and self-sufficient, and refused to be changed. Doing so only disqualified them from being used by God. Jesus wants to make us whole, clean and new. Are you willing to tell Jesus that you need his help? Is your pride or self-sufficiency getting in the way? Are you willing to be completely changed by him?

Jesus needs new people (vs 36–39)

As the Pharisees increasingly resisted the gospel, Jesus realised that they failed to understand the true gospel message. Just as a patch of new cloth would tear the old, and just as new wine would burst the old wineskin, Jesus' message and that of the Pharisees conflicted and could not exist together. As the church becomes absorbed in its traditions, it needs to remember this principle. If a church becomes bound by its traditions and comes into conflict with God's new work, it may lose its right to be God's instrument. We must constantly devote our hearts to Jesus so that he can transform us. Do you need to have your heart renewed by the Holy Spirit today? Are you bound by traditions?

Prayer: Lord, continually renew me by your Spirit that I may be worthy to be used by you.

Lord of the Sabbath

Beware of the dangers of legalism.

LUKE 6:1–11

Main verse: 'Then Jesus said to them, "The Son of Man is Lord of the Sabbath."'

Listen to the clear Word of God (vs 1–5)

God's law clearly states that God's people should keep the Sabbath day holy for God. Jesus kept God's law. If he had failed to keep even one small detail of God's law, he would have sinned and would have been unable to die in our place. What Jesus did not do, however, was to submit to the misinterpretations men made of God's law. This led to constant conflict between Jesus and the Pharisees on the issue of the Sabbath day. The Pharisees had made endless lists of what was permissible and what was not permissible on the Sabbath. Most of these rules had no basis in God's law. Jesus based his own actions on the Word of God. How do you view the Sabbath day? Have you submitted yourself to God's Word, or have you been trapped by people's misinterpretations of God's law?

Remember the mercy of God (vs 6–11)

Jesus' view of the Sabbath was based on the character of God. It would have been merciless to wait for the next day to heal the man's shrivelled arm. The Pharisees did, in fact, permit animals to be helped on the Sabbath but forbade the healing of a human being. For them, strict obedience to misinterpreted law was more important than showing love and mercy to hurting people. Jesus affirmed that acts of mercy and grace to suffering people were permissible on the Sabbath day. Yet the self-righteous attitude of the Pharisees soon revealed itself as they began to plot different ways to get rid of Jesus (v 11). Their very anger and plotting were in violation of God's law. We need to beware of how a legalistic attitude can blind us to overlook God's original intentions.

Prayer: Lord, free me from legalistic traditions and allow me to live sincerely what your Word teaches.

Jesus calls his disciples

If Jesus calls you, he will equip you.

LUKE 6:12–19

Main verse: 'When morning came, he called his disciples to him and chose twelve of them, whom he also designated apostles.'

Jesus chooses his disciples (vs 12–16)

At this time in Jesus' ministry, he chose a small group of men to train up as leaders of his work. He did not choose them hastily but prayerfully, after spending a night in prayer with his Father. We need to follow his example carefully when we select new leaders for our church. The most important thing is to seek the will of God. After an evening in prayer Jesus made his choice of twelve men. He chose with utmost care. Every day we are faced with the challenge to follow him or turn away. Has Jesus called you to a specific task for his kingdom? How are you doing? Do you need to reaffirm your commitment to that calling?

Jesus trains by example (vs 17–19)

We can be sure of two things when Jesus calls us to his work. First of all, he will be with us. Having called the twelve disciples, Jesus took them with him. He remained with them, whether in the flesh or in Spirit. Second, he trains those he has called. Jesus' training method is by example. Soon after Jesus chose his disciples, he ministered to needy people. The twelve disciples had the privilege of hearing his teachings and observing at first-hand how he healed the sick and cast out demons. What great training they received! Though we do not have the privilege of this same first-hand training, we can be absolutely certain that Jesus' calling means Jesus' equipping. Are you prepared for his call? Can you take immediate action as the Lord calls you to his service?

Prayer: Lord, grant me the willingness to learn from your faithful servants so that I may serve you better.

True prosperity
Spiritual blessings last forever.

LUKE 6:20-26

Main verse: 'Rejoice in that day and leap for joy, because great is your reward in heaven. For that is how their fathers treated the prophets.'

Eternal blessing (vs 20–23)

True blessing is spiritual blessing. When people pray for blessings, many tend to wish for material blessings. Jesus has a very different idea as to what true blessing meant. The highest blessing is eternal. True blessing is belonging to the kingdom of God. It may mean having less materially, but having Jesus reign in your heart will bring a deeper sense of joy and meaning to your life. True blessing results in satisfaction; your heart will know real joy. True blessing results in your identification with Jesus in his suffering. Such blessing might bring persecution into your life. But the wonderful thing is that such blessing will last forever. Do you want this kind of blessing? Are you prepared to pay the cost?

Temporary blessing (vs 24–26)

Every day we are faced with a choice. We have to choose between temporal and eternal things. Of course, Jesus is not saying that the rich can't be saved; his point is that those who devote themselves to accumulating riches will only know temporary satisfaction and lack eternal comfort. Similarly, those who devote themselves to eating and drinking will be physically full but spiritually empty. Those who live for the moment and who want simply to enjoy themselves now, face an eternity of unhappiness. Finally, those who seek the approval and praises of men may well find that they have sacrificed the more satisfying praise and approval of God. Which will you choose – temporary blessing or eternal blessing?

Prayer: Lord, create in me a thirst for the real and eternal blessings over temporary blessing.

Love your enemies

Show your love in some practical way to your enemy today.

LUKE 6:27–36

Main verse: 'But love your enemies, do good to them, and lend to them without expecting to get anything back. Then your reward will be great, and you will be sons of the Most High, because he is kind to the ungrateful and wicked.'

Show your love in action (vs 27–31)

Often our behaviour speaks louder than what we say with our lips. Normally we fight back against those who hurt us, yet Jesus demands a higher standard from his followers. Christians must be different. Instead of hurting our enemies, he tells us to be good to them (v 27). He wants us to pray for them (v 28). He asks us to persevere in times of persecution. He wants us to be detached from our material possessions, to avoid getting upset if they are stolen and never returned. Jesus expects his people to express their love not just in words but also in deeds. What is your attitude and actions toward your enemies? Is there someone who has hurt you recently that you need to forgive and pray for today?

Be different for Jesus (vs 32–36)

People's lives are completely exposed before God's eyes, but they can be deceptive to the human eye. Jesus said that even sinners are able to express love towards those who love them (v 32). They are able to do good to those who do good to them (v 33). They are even able to lend money to those in need – but expect to get it back in full again (v 34). Yet a Christian must transcend this standard of the world. Encouraging us to imitate him, Jesus tells us to fix our eyes on the reward we will receive in heaven. He also reminds us that we are children of God and that our heavenly Father is a merciful God. Does Christ's love motivate you to embrace those who are against you?

Prayer: Merciful Father, just as you have shown forgiveness, love and mercy to me, help me to express loving mercy to someone who has hurt me.

How to live together in Jesus

Treat others as you wish to be treated.

LUKE 6:37–42

Main verse: 'Give, and it will be given to you. A good measure, pressed down, shaken together and running over, will be poured into your lap. For with the measure you use, it will be measured to you.'

Be generous in spirit (vs 37,38)

People usually receive what they give. The kind of people who point out faults in others usually draw much criticism to themselves. Those who constantly condemn and discourage others can't but expect to receive accusations and discouragement themselves. People who hold fierce grudges against those who have hurt them find it difficult to receive forgiveness from others. However, those who are willing to forgive others can expect to be forgiven when they make mistakes. Also, cheerful givers who generously offer their time and resources can expect to receive much. In what ways do you need to be more generous? Have you been quick to hold grudges while slow to forgive?

Recognise your own faults (vs 39–42)

One of the problems most people face is the blindness to their own faults. Everyone is quick to see faults in others, yet our sinful nature tends to overlook our own faults. Therefore Jesus warns us to see the serious faults existing in our own lives before pointing out those in others (v 41). We must accept the help of others, yet we need to be selective in who leads us. Choosing people who are as blind as ourselves will result in simply falling with them. In order to accept the guidance of others, we need to have a humble and willing spirit to learn. What are some of the 'planks' in your eye? Have you been neglecting to deal with hypocrisy in your own life?

Prayer: Lord, please help me see my own flaws, that I may be as honest with others as I want them to be with me.

Build on a good foundation

A pure heart and a good foundation are essential for good Christian living.

LUKE 6:43–49

Main verse: 'He is like a man building a house, who dug down deep and laid the foundation on rock. When the flood came, the torrent struck that house but could not shake it, because it was well built.'

A pure heart (vs 43–45)

Godly life depends, first of all, on having a pure heart. Good intention and conduct spring from your heart. An evil heart will produce evil fruit; a good heart produces good fruit (v 45). So before you can please God, you must be born again by the Spirit of God and receive from him a new heart, a clean heart. One can discern whether a person is regenerated by the fruit he bears (v 44). If a person is truly born again, manifestations of a new, transformed life will become evident. What kind of fruit is being produced in your life? Can others know that you are a Christian by the fruit you bear? How is your heart today?

A good foundation (vs 46–49)

Verbal confession alone is insufficient to demonstrate that you are a Christian. It is often too easy to say with your lips that Jesus is your Lord. In order to build your life on solid foundation there are three things you need to do. First, you must come to Jesus. Second, you need to hear his Word. Third, and most importantly, you must apply his Word into practice. Hearing God's Word is not enough; memorising God's Word is not enough. Life's solid foundation is built and developed when God's Word is actively exercised in your life. When you are obedient to the transforming power of God's Word, you can resist every storm. From today's passage, what do you need to practice? How would you evaluate the 'foundation' you are currently building upon?

Prayer: Lord, renew my heart daily and help me to build a firm foundation in my life by obedience to your Word.

Great faith

Jesus' command carries healing power.

LUKE 7:1–10

Main verse: 'For I myself am a man under authority, with soldiers under me. I tell this one, "Go", and he goes; and that one, "Come", and he comes. I say to my servant, "Do this", and he does it.'

A good man (vs 1–5)

The centurion in this story was a remarkable man. He showed genuine concern in his servants' problems and treated his servants with respect. Moreover, he respected the Jewish religion. He loved the Jews and helped them in any way he could. Evidently he sought after the truth and recognised the God of the Jews as the real sovereign God. Although the Jewish people have not always lived up to God's expectations, they remain as the chosen people of God. People praised this centurion for his good nature; he was a well-liked man. What kind of employer are you? Do you sincerely care about those who work for you or with you?

A believing man (vs 6–10)

We see two other remarkable features of this centurion. The first is his humility. He was a Roman – one of the people who ruled the world – and yet he did not consider himself worthy to come before Jesus (vs 6,7). People thought he deserved Jesus' assistance, but he thought otherwise (vs 4,5). No one deserves the mercy of Jesus, but he freely bestows it. The most remarkable feature of this man was his faith. He believed that Jesus needed only to speak the word and his servant would be healed (v 7). He believed in the power of Jesus' words; Jesus' presence was not required. He did not demand Jesus' healing touch but simply asked for Jesus' command to heal. Is your faith firmly rooted in the power of God's Word, or do you need concrete evidence before you can believe? How are you challenged by the centurion's walk by faith?

Prayer: Lord, bestow upon me a faith that will simply believe in the power of your Word.

Raised to life

Jesus is the Lord of life and death.

LUKE 7:11–17

Main verse: 'The dead man sat up and began to talk, and Jesus gave him back to his mother.'

Jesus – filled with compassion (vs 11–13)

Death is a consequence of sin. It is the destroyer of relationships and the breaker of hearts. When Jesus saw the widow accompanying the dead body of her only son, he had compassion on her (v 13). He probably imagined how her life would be led as a single person. The depth of her tragedy was emphasised by the large crowd who accompanied her. But would those people be near her to help in the coming weeks? It was doubtful. Thankfully, Jesus doesn't wait to be asked to get involved in our problems. He takes the initiative, hearing and answering our prayers before we can even ask. He has come to be with us in our sorrow, to wipe away our tears. He has promised that one day there will be no more tears for his people. If you're going through a time of pain, will you invite Jesus' compassion into your life today?

Jesus – conqueror of death (vs 14–17)

We have already seen that Jesus' word was powerful enough to defeat illness and to bring healing. In verses 14 and 15, we see that his word even conquered death itself. If Jesus was unable to deal with the problem of death, then his ultimate accomplishment would have failed. Jesus exhibited his ability to deal with the problem of our sin by overcoming this boy's death. Jesus proved himself to be the Lord of life and death. No wonder people speculated about Jesus' identity. Although their understanding was limited, they realised that God had indeed entered into their world and shown concern for their deepest needs. Do you believe that God is greater than your problems?

Prayer: Lord, thank you that I never need to be afraid of death because you have conquered it for me.

Dealing with doubt

Trust in the Word of God without doubting.

LUKE 7:18–23

Main verse: 'So he replied to the messengers, "Go back and report to John what you have seen and heard: The blind receive sight, the lame walk, those who have leprosy are cured, the deaf hear, the dead are raised, and the good news is preached to the poor."'

Take your doubts to Jesus (vs 18–20)

Even the best of God's servants can be subject to periods of discouragement and doubt. It seems that Jesus did not fulfil all the expectations which John had in mind for the Messiah. John might have been influenced by most people's expectation of the Messiah as a political figure. It was possible he was in prison at that time and that his current circumstances caused doubts to arise in his mind. Such a fearful experience could well have undermined his faith and caused him to waver. However, John handled his doubts well by addressing them to Jesus, who is able to deal with all of our doubts. Do you sometimes have doubts about Jesus?

Place your faith in him (vs 21–23)

In dealing with John's doubts, Jesus responds to him in three ways. First of all, he directs John's vision to his activities. He points John to the signs and wonders which testify of Jesus' identity. Secondly, he refers John to the Scriptures. His answer was couched in the words of Isaiah 61:1. He reminds John that the Scriptures must be the source of his faith. Only the teaching of the Bible will dispel our doubts. Finally, Jesus does not condemn John for his doubts – to have done so would have driven him into deeper discouragement. Rather, he encourages him to believe and to remain steadfast. Will you be honest about your doubts, as God will be faithful and honest with you?

Prayer: Lord, I bring my doubts honestly to you, so that you can help me to believe with strong convictions.

Greater than John

What does it mean to be least in the kingdom of God?

LUKE 7:24-35

Main verse: 'I tell you, among those born of women there is no one greater than John; yet the one who is least in the kingdom of God is greater than he.'

Know Jesus (vs 24-28)

As soon as John's messengers left, Jesus sought to restore the reputation of John the Baptist. When the people had previously flocked to the desert, it wasn't simply to enjoy the scenery or to see someone dressed in beautiful clothes. They had gone to the desert to hear a man who claimed to speak for God, to hear a prophet of God. According to Jesus there was no prophet as great as John the Baptist (v 28). Jesus uplifts those who are downcast; he restores those who have fallen. Jesus encourages all his followers to rise above even John the Baptist. Are there times when you belittle yourself before God? Have you forgotten who you are in Christ?

Repent and believe (vs 29-35)

Those who had already submitted themselves in repentance, and who had accepted the baptism from John, opened their hearts to the Lord Jesus. They understood and believed who he was and what he taught. On the other hand, the religious leaders who had refused to repent and submit to John's baptism also rejected Jesus. No matter what Jesus did, they distorted Jesus' teaching and actions to suit their own point of view. John was condemned as demonic for abstaining from food; Jesus was condemned as a glutton for eating freely. The truth is clear. Before anyone can come to know Jesus, he must submit in repentance to Jesus. As he humbles himself before the Lord, his pride will be broken. The first step is repentance. Have you something to repent to the Lord?

Prayer: Lord, because you have declared me righteous based on the forgiveness of my sins, I wish to follow John's example and serve you faithfully.

Repentance needs to be seen

Those who are forgiven much will love Jesus much.

LUKE 7:36–50

Main verse: 'Therefore, I tell you, her many sins have been forgiven – for she loved much. But he who has been forgiven little loves little.'

A sinner reaches out to Jesus (vs 36–38)
Although the woman in this story hadn't heard the words of forgiveness from Jesus, she knew he would accept her despite her sinful past. He would forgive her. She expressed her belief in his forgiveness by her humility. She stood behind Jesus for she felt unworthy to stand in front of Jesus. Her belief was also expressed in her tears, which symbolised sorrow over sins of the past (v 38). Her act of love was also an expression of her repentance, her desire to change. Supremely her faith was expressed in her gratitude, offering to Jesus the most lavish and expensive gift she possessed. In what ways have you expressed your repentance and faith in Jesus? How does this woman's love for Jesus move you to greater obedience and love?

Jesus reaches out to a sinner (vs 39–50)
Although Simon, the Pharisee, invited Jesus to his home for dinner, his motives are questionable. We can speculate that Simon intended to insult Jesus since he deprived him of the common courtesies normally given to guests – washing feet, welcoming with a kiss and anointing guests with oil. For Jesus, however, an insult would not keep him from reaching out to a lost man. Like most of us, Simon was quick to notice the sins of others but was blind to his own. Through Jesus, he was finally left with the unmistakable message that forgiveness of sin is possible only through confession and repentance. Do you withhold adoration for Jesus?

Prayer: Lord, awaken me to see the extent of my sinful ways and receive your forgiveness through repentance.

The fruit of the word

With your willingness, God's Word will bear fruit.

LUKE 8:1-8

Main verse: '"Still other seed fell on good soil. It came up and yielded a crop, a hundred times more than was sown." When he said this, he called out, "He who has ears to hear, let him hear."'

Expect results (vs 1–3)

Jesus wanted the gospel to be heard by everyone. The gospel that Jesus proclaimed was good news because it established the kingdom of God. It was a gospel of power over evil and sickness. The gospel brought the rule of God over people's lives; many people who followed Jesus' ministry were living proofs of the gospel's life-changing message. Their lives were a testimony to the healing from disease and freedom from evil spirits. The gospel Jesus proclaimed was for all people, from the highest in society to the lowest. When it had come to take root in the lives of men and women, it resulted in an increased desire to follow Jesus wherever he went and a willingness to live for God's kingdom. What changes has the gospel brought into your life?

Listen carefully (vs 4–8)

Every seed has potential to bear fruit, but the result will depend on the type of soil (or heart) into which the seed falls. Everywhere the gospel was proclaimed, various results were produced. In some cases the results were minimal but in other cases the results were enormous. For those of us who share the message of the gospel with others, we can be assured that certain results will follow. It is the submission to the Word of God that changes lives. That is, if we long to bear fruit for God, we need to listen carefully and attentively, and prepare to live obediently. How attentively are you listening to God?

Prayer: Lord, I yearn for a transformed life to bear much fruit for your kingdom. I utterly rely on you to accomplish this task.

How the word bears fruit

Good soil produces good crop.

LUKE 8:9–15

Main verse: 'But the seed on good soil stands for those with a noble and good heart, who hear the word, retain it, and by persevering produce a crop.'

Don't reject the Word (vs 9,10)

Jesus' parables can be taken merely as simple stories designed to make his teaching easier to comprehend. However, they contain profound insights into God's kingdom. Jesus desires his followers to have their spiritual eyes opened. Those who follow him will be given more understanding; but for people who have rejected him, there is the agony of hearing the Word yet being unable to understand it. Many people hear the Word without comprehension, for God has not opened their minds and hearts to it. There is nothing more terrifying than judgement from God and being cut off from the primary source of salvation. Is your mind open to the Word of God? Are your spiritual eyes opened to God's truth?

Receive the Word (vs 11–15)

Hearing God's Word is not enough. It must be received and planted in our hearts if it is to bear good fruit. There are people who hear the Word but refuse its influence on their lives. The devil is eager to prevent the Word from taking effect on us. Unfortunately, some people can listen to God's Word with no intention of allowing it to change their lives. Then there are others who receive the Word but are too engrossed in their worries and taken up in their pursuit of riches and pleasures to allow it to transform their lives. In these cases the Word becomes ineffective. Only those who hear the Word, keep it close to their hearts and apply it will bear good fruit. How teachable is your heart today? Is it ready to produce a crop?

Prayer: Lord, may I have greater love for your Word each day by having a heart that is receptive and obedient.

Listen and believe

Listening to the Word of God and believing it are essential to a life of blessing.

LUKE 8:16-25

Main verse: 'Therefore consider carefully how you listen. Whoever has will be given more; whoever does not have, even what he thinks he has will be taken from him.'

A test of listening (vs 16–21)
The results of listening to God's Word can be quite costly, yet the rewards are immense. God's Word is like a light which shines in our hearts to expose any hidden sin (v 17). This exposure of sin is painful but necessary for evil to be rooted out of our hearts. When God's Word works in our hearts, we are led into a deeper understanding of both God and ourselves, and into fuller blessing. God desires to bless us abundantly by removing sins from our lives as we confess them to him. For those of us who gladly receive the Word of God, there awaits the tremendous privilege of being counted as one of the closest family members of Jesus Christ. For Jesus, those closest to him were not necessarily those of his earthly family but rather those who submitted to the will of God (v 21). Are you listening with an open heart to God's Word?

A test of faith (vs 22–25)
How deeply tired Jesus must have been to have fallen asleep in the boat and to sleep through the great storm which arose. Here, we see Jesus' sense of peace and security knowing that the Heavenly Father was in control. The disciples still had much to learn. They had to understand that fixing their eyes on the storms and dangers of life will only create fear. Instead, they needed to learn that Jesus' presence casts out any fear, that Jesus was greater than any danger they would face. Anything is possible with Jesus. Are you feeling swamped these days? Where are your eyes focused? Where have you put your ultimate trust?

Prayer: Almighty God, purify me from my iniquities and lead me to grow stronger in faith.

Jesus deals with evil spirits

Jesus wants us to be freed from the influence of evil.

LUKE 8:26–39

Main verse: 'And the people went out to see what had happened. When they came to Jesus, they found the man from whom the demons had gone out, sitting at Jesus' feet, dressed and in his right mind; and they were afraid.'

Bound by Satan (vs 26–33)

Satan is in the business of destroying lives. He seeks to control us and bring us into submission to himself. The man in this story lived a life of madness and loneliness. His life was characterised by violence, and he spent his days in the presence of death. But upon meeting Jesus, his life was changed. Satan never gives up willingly, and in this case, the demons pled with Jesus not to be sent to the Abyss (v 31). Even demons knew that they would be defeated and sent to a place of eternal condemnation. Jesus sent them into the pigs as a living demonstration that the demon-possessed man was set free. This demonstrated Jesus' sovereign power over the demons and the ultimate fate of Satan. Do you believe in the power of Jesus?

Freed by Jesus (vs 34–39)

Jesus brought a drastic change into this man's life. From a life of restlessness, nakedness and derangement, the man was transformed by Jesus. He sat peacefully, fully clothed and sane at Jesus' feet. Because the transformation in the man's life was so incredible, observers were in awe before such demonstration of power. They were faced with a choice. They could submit to the One who had power to defeat evil, or they could give in to their fears and reject the Almighty One. Sadly, these people decided that Jesus was too intimidating to live with, and they asked him to leave. The demon-possessed man, however, chose differently. He wanted to be with Jesus. Does Jesus' power free you from bondages in your life?

Prayer: God, I need your strength to be free from all evil. Let me walk close to you today.

Healed by a touch

Jesus has different ways to meet our needs.

LUKE 8:40-48

Main verse: 'She came up behind him and touched the edge of his cloak, and immediately her bleeding stopped.'

Don't be afraid to ask (vs 40–42)

After the rejection that Jesus experienced from the people of Gesarenes, he was received back to Galilee with a warm welcome. A man named Jairus seized the opportunity to meet Jesus, pleading with him to come and heal his daughter who was dying. For some people, like the centurion in chapter 7, Jesus' words were enough to bring about healing, but others, like Jairus, desperately yearned for his presence before the dying child. Jesus often graciously accommodates himself to our level of faith. Yet Jesus freely takes opportunities to test and strengthen our faith. Will you remain faithful despite seeming delays by Jesus? What opportunities have you been given recently that strengthen and test your faith?

Don't be afraid to come (vs 43–48)

This woman must have been consumed with many fearful thoughts. Her illness had precluded her for twelve years from going to the temple to worship God. She had experienced much rejection by others; people believed that everything she touched became unclean. If the crowd knew of her disease, they would have lynched her for getting too close to them. Jesus was on his way to heal the daughter of an important and religious man; surely he couldn't spare time for her? With these deep-rooted fears within her, she reached out in faith to touch Jesus' garment. Despite her past rejection and pain, she had great faith in Jesus. She believed in his healing touch. Not only did she learn of Jesus' power, but of his full compassion for her. Have you ever known Jesus' power? His compassion?

Prayer: Lord Jesus, thank you for your concern in me and in my struggles. Realising your willingness to take time for me, I bow down before you in gratitude.

Just believe

You must believe in Jesus despite uncertainties.

LUKE 8:49–56

Main verse: 'Hearing this, Jesus said to Jairus, "Don't be afraid; just believe, and she will be healed."'

Don't be afraid (vs 49,50)

It must have been frustrating for Jairus when Jesus took time with the bleeding woman while the news arrived to inform him of his daughter's death. Although it is not expressed, Jairus could have resented Jesus for the delay which prevented him from healing his daughter in time. Confronted with the sad news, Jesus is quick to share words of faith, comfort and hope. No matter how hopeless a situation may seem, there is always hope with Jesus. Jairus had already set his hopes on the presence of Jesus. He had already believed that Jesus could heal his daughter - now he had to trust Jesus to raise his daughter from the dead. Jesus gives us opportunities to increase our faith. How is your faith today?

Only believe (vs 51–56)

When Jesus arrived at Jairus' home, many people were weeping and wailing for the child's death. Interestingly, Jesus said that she was 'sleeping', which shows that God's ways and understanding are different from ours. His power is operative even before we seek it. We must be careful of allowing doubt and unbelief to overtake us. Unbelief is very destructive, killing even the smallest seed of faith in our hearts. This explains Jesus' refusal to allow anyone else but two of his closest disciples and the parents into the room where the girl was laid. Dispelling unbelief, Jesus uttered the words of faith and the child was brought back to life. Have you allowed your faith to be influenced by unbelievers? Is your faith hindered by the world's understanding of circumstances?

Prayer: Merciful God, be gracious when I question my faith in you. Help me to trust your Word with all my heart and all my mind.

Equipped to serve

Jesus equips you for the task he has given you.

LUKE 9:1–9

Main verse: 'When Jesus had called the twelve together, he gave them power and authority to drive out all demons and to cure diseases'.

Go with the gospel (vs 1–6)
The time had come for Jesus' disciples to learn beyond listening and observing. It was time for them to see that they had been empowered to do the very things which Jesus had been doing. Before Jesus calls us to do anything for him, he prepares and equips us to fulfil the task. Jesus gave his disciples authority and power to preach, to heal and to cast out demons. Jesus also encouraged them to take nothing with them (v 3). This action was so that they might demonstrate their faith in God's full provision. They were also sent out with a sense of urgency. They were not to waste time with people who rejected the gospel (v 5). They took on their mission, sharing the gospel throughout the villages. Is it time now for you to proclaim the gospel publicly?

Expect reactions (vs 7–9)
Proclaiming the gospel often produces unexpected reactions in people. When the disciples proclaimed the gospel publicly, people began to talk and speculate. The gospel proclaimed and the miracles performed became the news of the day. For Herod, this news brought uneasiness about his act of beheading John the Baptist. As the stories of Jesus spread among the people, Herod's interest in him increased. Perhaps deep in his heart he wanted forgiveness. But it is not enough to feel guilty for our sin; one must come to a genuine repentance. Herod missed his chance because he rejected the gospel. Will you start praying for boldness to respond to people's reactions and inquiries about the gospel of Jesus?

Prayer: Lord, wherever I am, equip me to witness boldly to the gospel of Jesus, knowing your presence with me.

The feeding of five thousand

In Jesus' presence and power you can do all things.

LUKE 9:10–17

Main verse: 'They all ate and were satisfied, and the disciples picked up twelve basketfuls of broken pieces that were left over.'

Jesus heals the sick (vs 10,11)

The disciples had discovered their empowerment in response to Jesus' command to proclaim the gospel. Most likely they were eager to spend time alone with Jesus to tell him about their adventure. But to be alone with Jesus was difficult because large crowds sought after him. Jesus demonstrated great patience and compassion for the crowds, and yet willingly sacrificed his private time with the disciples to meet their needs. Jesus consistently spoke about the kingdom of God and demonstrated his power over sickness and disease. Are you willing to sacrifice your personal time for the sake of gospel?

Jesus feeds the people (vs 12–17)

The disciples were successful in healing the sick and casting out demons. Yet when they returned to Jesus, they seemed helpless. When they were faced with the problem of feeding five thousand people, they exhibited utter despair (v 13). They seemed to have forgotten the power and authority Jesus had given them (vs 1,2). He challenged them: 'You give them something to eat' (v 13). The disciples discovered that in obedience to the command of Jesus, they were able to provide. Do you realise that Jesus' call to obedience is also his promise for provision? As the disciples distributed the bread and fish, the miracle took place before their very eyes. This resulted in feeding everyone sufficiently with plenty left over. What is Jesus calling you to obey today?

Prayer: Lord, thank you for the power and authority you have given me to live according to your command.

You are the Christ

What you are as a disciple is directly related to who Jesus is.

LUKE 9:18-27

Main verse: 'And he said, "The Son of Man must suffer many things and be rejected by the elders, chief priests and teachers of the law, and he must be killed and on the third day be raised to life."'

Who is Jesus? (vs 18–22)

People had various ideas about Jesus' identity. Some thought he was John the Baptist, Elijah or another Old Testament prophet brought back to life from the dead. Inspired by the Holy Spirit, it was Peter who declared Jesus' true identity (v 20). He was the Messiah – the anticipated Christ. Though Peter's reply was correct, we need to question whether his conception of the Messiah coincided with what Jesus embodied. Jesus defined his identity and purpose as the Messiah who was to suffer and die (v 22). He was to be resurrected in order to have victory over sin and death. Becoming disciples of Jesus requires understanding of who he is. Who do you believe Jesus is?

Who are his disciples? (vs 23–27)

Jesus demands absolute commitment from his disciples. As true disciples, we must give all of ourselves to Christ, including our plans, our desires, even our preferences. Jesus will not ask you to do more than you can handle. A true disciple follows Jesus even though it may require going through unwanted experiences. A true disciple denies herself, relinquishing things which could become stumbling blocks in obeying God's will. A true disciple takes up his cross daily, and crucifies his fleshly nature. A true disciple gladly offers her life for Jesus, and is not ashamed of Jesus' words. Do you consider yourself to be a true disciple? How must you take up his cross today? Will you take that step towards wholehearted commitment?

Prayer: Lord, I desire to know you more intimately each day. Let my life be a profession and reflection of the Messiah.

A transforming experience

Seeking God will lead you into deeper experiences with him.

LUKE 9:28-36

Main verse: 'As he was praying, the appearance of his face changed, and his clothes became as bright as a flash of lightning.'

A glimpse of his glory (vs 28–33)

Jesus' three closest disciples had a revealing glimpse of their Master. By their experience on the mountain, the disciples learned that prayer stimulates tremendous changes. As Jesus prayed, he was transformed in appearance right before their very eyes. On that day they learned that Jesus was much more than he appeared to be; they caught a vision of the glorious Jesus that others weren't privileged to see. Next, through the conversation Jesus had with Moses and Elijah, the disciples better understood God's eternal plan concerning Jesus Christ. Are you convinced that seeking the Lord's face will lead you to a glorious relationship with him? Do you need to reorganise your priorities these days to seek him?

A private experience (vs 34–36)

Before this whole experience was over there were still some truths to be learned. When God grants one to witness a special revelation of himself, there will be fear and trembling that accompanies the holiness of God. But this very holy God desires personal fellowship with his children, constantly expressing his love for them. There are some experiences we receive from God which are private and are not to be shared with others; God covets private moments with each person. They are just for God and us. It is wise to keep those special times hidden from others, especially if those experiences with God cause you to become spiritually proud. Do you understand what it means to fear God? Are you convinced of his special love for you?

Prayer: Lord, continue to show me the fullness of your character while teaching me to be ever humble before you.

The consequences of unbelief

Unbelief leads us to failure, despair and confusion.

LUKE 9:37–45

Main verse: 'Even while the boy was coming, the demon threw him to the ground in a convulsion. But Jesus rebuked the evil spirit, healed the boy and gave him back to his father.'

The failure of unbelief (vs 37–41)

The three disciples had little opportunity to enjoy their mountain-top experience with Jesus before they found themselves faced with the realities of living in a sinful world. The disciples successfully drove demons out in the past. They were empowered by Jesus. However, in this case they had failed. Had they forgotten their previous triumph? Had they yielded to jealousy over being left behind while the other three prayed with Jesus? Were they too afraid? According to Jesus, their unbelief was the only reason for failure. There are no limits to what can be accomplished by God through faith. Has your faith been growing or weakening in recent days? Why?

The blindness of unbelief (vs 42–45)

Jesus was not overtaken by the tactics of the demon. Rather, he took firm control over the situation and at once cast out the demon, healed the boy to normal condition and restored him to his father (v 42). It is a vivid example of his mission on earth – to establish freedom, healing and restoration. The people were astonished by Jesus' power; however, they could not understand what they had just witnessed in the light of greater events to come (v 45). Unbelief blinded their minds to the truth about Jesus. We must submit our minds to the Word of God so that he can lead us to believe who Jesus is. What have you learned today that strengthens your faith in Jesus?

Prayer: Lord, strengthen my faith in you, for I commit my frailties into your hands.

Who is the greatest?

Imitating Jesus means being humble and merciful.

LUKE 9:46–56

Main verse: 'Whoever welcomes this little child in my name welcomes me; and whoever welcomes me welcomes the one who sent me. For he who is least among you all – he is the greatest.'

Learn to be humble (vs 46–48)

The disciples still had much to learn before Jesus left them. He tried to warn them about his death, but they were more concerned about which of them would obtain high positions in the kingdom of God (v 46). Jesus tells them that the values of his kingdom are very different from the values of the world. In his kingdom, the greatest would be the humblest (v 48). The greatest would welcome the smallest, the weakest and the least important people into their lives, and gladly take the lowest place. Our real commitment towards Jesus is revealed in the way we treat others whom he loves. Are you striving after the greatness the world offers, or after true greatness that results from submission to Jesus?

Learn to be accepting (vs 49–56)

Two incidents portrayed here reveal our narrowness and intolerance compared to Jesus' goodness and mercy. First, when the disciples heard of a man driving out demons in Jesus' name, they wanted to stop him. In light of their recent failure to do likewise, perhaps jealousy motivated their reaction. Perhaps they could not bear the fact that God would use someone else. How do you react when God is blessing another person or church or group more than your own? The second incident occurred when villagers refused to welcome Jesus (v 53). Whereas the disciples condemned them, Jesus showed acceptance regarding the situation. Are you quick to condemn others who are different, or are you prepared to listen and even accept them?

Prayer: Lord, teach me the true meaning of greatness in your kingdom as you work in me an attitude of humility.

Follow me

To follow Jesus, he must be first.

LUKE 9:57–62

Main verse: 'Jesus replied, "No one who puts his hand to the plough and looks back is fit for service in the kingdom of God."'

Count the cost (vs 57,58)
The first man in this story willingly offered to follow Jesus. We are quick to make promises without seriously considering the cost or the consequences of what we are saying. Before Jesus accepts the man's offer, he challenges him to face the cost of his action (v 58). To follow Jesus, he must be prepared to lead a life with no possessions, with no permanent dwelling place. Jesus' followers must be prepared to go anywhere Jesus calls them. Upon Jesus' command, they must give up everything for him. To say we will follow Jesus and to actually do so are often two different things. If Jesus called you to give up your home, your family, your career for him, would you be prepared to do so?

Don't make excuses (vs 59–62)
Jesus invited the second man to follow him, but it is not clear whether the third man responded to the same invitation. Clearly, though, each had an excuse and condition to the call to obedience. The second man wanted to wait until his father died before he followed Jesus. The third man wished to resolve family matters before he left them. Jesus is not interested in partially-committed obedience; he wants all that we have. He does not want people who are constantly looking back and hankering after things they have left behind. He seeks people who are fully committed to him. Do you have any excuses? What limitations have you put on your obedience to God?

Prayer: Lord Jesus, forgive my unwillingness to pay the cost of living for you. May my obedience have no restrictions.

Go with the gospel

Jesus calls his workers to join the harvesting.

LUKE 10:1–16

Main verse: 'He told them, "The harvest is plentiful, but the workers are few. Ask the Lord of the harvest, therefore, to send out workers into his harvest field."'

Preach the gospel of peace (vs 1–9)

The time had come for the disciples to get practical training. Jesus fully equipped them and sent them out in pairs to encourage and complement one another for the work ahead. He promised to follow up on all they did. They were to prepare the way for Jesus. He promised that they would see a harvest for their labour despite some opposition they would confront along the way. They were instructed to take nothing so that they could completely trust in Jesus' provision. Jesus wanted them to learn contentment beyond circumstances and to show fairness to all. Their main mission, however, was to proclaim a gospel of peace to as many people as possible. Are you prepared to proclaim the gospel, trusting in Jesus' full provision?

Preach the warning of judgement (vs 10–16)

If the gospel was rejected, the disciples were to shake the dust off their feet and to warn the people that in rejecting their gospel, they were rejecting Jesus and ultimately God himself (vs 11,16). Rejecting the gospel will lead to the judgement of God. Keep in mind that the people in the villages had several opportunities to hear the gospel. There comes a time when people must move on to share the gospel with others who are more responsive. Rejecting the gospel brings drastic consequences (vs 12–15). How are you challenged to be more bold in evangelism? Will you make it your prayer focus today?

Prayer: Dear Jesus, your good news truly brings peace into people's lives. By your boldness, I pray to proclaim the gospel without fear.

Rejoice in the right things

Jesus came that we might have abundant joy.

LUKE 10:17–24

Main verse: 'However, do not rejoice that the spirits submit to you, but rejoice that your names are written in heaven.'

The disciples rejoice (vs 17–20)

From the very beginning, Satan has been a defeated foe. Jesus witnessed the attempted rebellion and defeat of Satan as he fell from heaven. Being above Satan, Jesus gives to his people power and authority over demons. The disciples rejoiced in their power to bring demons into submission, but Jesus forbids his disciples to misunderstand that power. Power can be very intoxicating; thus he counsels them not to rejoice in their power, but rather to rejoice in the fact that God has saved them by his grace and has written their names in the book of heaven (v 20). Have you taken credit or boasted in your strength lately? What gives you most joy in this life?

Jesus rejoices (vs 21–24)

Jesus had many things in which he rejoiced. First of all, he found joy in the Holy Spirit (v 21). Also, he found joy in the way God so often reveals his grace in unexpected and beautiful ways. Jesus was delighted that God had revealed heavenly knowledge not to the wise and the learned of the world but to the young and foolish. Those who have been cast aside and ignored by the world are the very ones who receive careful and personal attention from God. Jesus also rejoiced in the unique and personal relationship he had with the Father (v 21). Finally, Jesus found joy in revealing to his chosen ones the truths about God. Do you rejoice in these things? Is your delight in your heavenly Father?

Prayer: Thank you for granting your divine joy, O Saviour. Show me how to rejoice in all things today.

Dynamic Bible resources from Scripture Union

Daily Bible reading from Scripture Union – suitable
for every age from pre-readers to pensioners

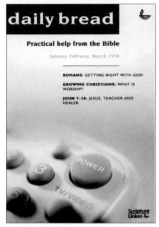

Daily Bread: Practical help from the Bible

Daily Bread helps people explore, understand and enjoy
the Bible – and work it out in everyday life. *Daily Bread*
gives you:

*   A Bible reading for each day
*   Easy to understand, practical comments, relating the
    Bible to everyday life.
*   Information panels to explain the world of the
    Bible.
*   Special 'Talkabout' section for individuals or small
    groups

Daily Bread is also available in large print format.

Published quarterly, £2.45 per issue.

April, May, June 1998

Encounter
with God

In depth Bible notes

John
Hosea
Ecclesiastes
Romans
Acts

Find rest, O my soul,
in God alone

Scripture
Union

Encounter with God: In-depth Bible notes

Encounter with God is designed for readers who want a
thoughtful, in-depth approach to systematic Bible reading.

- Daily consecutive Bible readings.
- Exposition by experienced Bible teachers.
- Introduction and review articles for each consecu-
  tive series, enabling further study, reflection and
  response.
- Feature articles, addressing contemporary issues.
- A dual programme, covering the Bible in either one
  or six years.

Published quarterly, £2.45 per issue.

Closer to God: Reading the Bible in the power of the Holy Spirit

Closer to God is for anyone who believes or hopes that God speaks to ordinary people: loving, freeing, changing and healing them in today's world. There's a Bible reading with notes for every day of the week but each weekly section is designed so that if you miss up to two days you still won't get behind.

Published every two months, £1.95 per issue

Alive to God: Creative reflections on the Bible

Alive to God encourages imaginative, thoughtful and reflective responses to scripture by providing:

• A framework for prayer, praise, reflection and action
• Systematic and thematic series
• Colour pages, photographs and a mini-poster for further meditation

Published quarterly, £2.45 per quarter

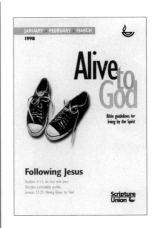

DAYZD (14s to 18s)

Each of the four books in the *DAYZD* series contains 90 days of undated Bible reading material. Each book has a two page feature section which focuses on the title theme – Relationships, Worship, Evangelism and Guidance.

Each book costs £2.50

One Up (11s to 14s)

One Up presents daily Bible readings in an up-to-date teen magazine format to which this age group can instantly relate. In full colour, with a problem page, cartoons and music reviews as well as a centre page feature on the issue of the quarter.

£2.20 per quarter.

Let's Go (7s to 9s)

A 48 page colour magazine to help this age group explore the Bible – stories are retold in the magazine as cartoon characters travel back in time to meet Bible characters. Puzzles, cartoons, crafts and lots of other absorbing activities reinforce the biblical theme.

Let's Go is published quarterly and costs £2.85

Check it Out! (9s to 11s)

The ultimate Bible reading guide for 9s to 11s, *Check it Out!* comes in a funfax format. Readers rip out pages from the quarterly booklet and file them in the mini-binder under sections such as Bible discovery, worship, maps, and diary. Actual page size: 170x115mm.

Each quarter costs £2.85

How can you inherit eternal life?

Show your love for God in deed as well as in word.

LUKE 10:25–37

Main verse: 'He answered, "'Love the Lord your God with all your heart and with all your soul and with all your strength and with all your mind'; and 'Love your neighbour as yourself'."'

Love God (vs 25–28)

An expert in the law asked the most important question in life, that is, how to inherit eternal life. Jesus answered him by referring him to the law itself. It is pertinent to know the continuity and harmony between the Old and the New Testaments. Both offer the same answer. That is to say, if you want to inherit eternal life, first and foremost you must love God. Eternal life begins with your relationship with God. You must commit yourself to him. You must love him wholeheartedly. Jesus reminds us that genuine love manifests itself in concrete, practical ways. Consequently, Jesus and the law of God teach us to love the Lord and to love our neighbour as ourselves. How do you express your love for God?

Love your neighbour (vs 29–37)

This lawyer wanted everything carefully defined, and prompted Jesus to explain what he means by 'neighbour'. In the following parable, Jesus tells us that a neighbour is someone who will not overlook another who desperately needs assistance. A neighbour does not hesitate to get personally involved. Regardless of the person's social status or racial background, a loving neighbour willingly offers himself to help another person. The Samaritan man gladly paid from his own pocket to secure this needy person's well-being. If we truly love God, then our love must find its expression in caring for others in need. Do you love your neighbour? In what practical ways do you show your love?

Prayer: Lord, I ask that my love for you will manifest itself in loving actions toward others.

Learn to listen

Set aside personal time to listen to the words of God.

LUKE 10:38–42

Main verse: 'She had a sister called Mary, who sat at the Lord's feet listening to what he said.'

Listen to God (vs 38,39)

Although Martha is often criticised in this story, remember that it was Martha who initially invited Jesus to her home. Without Martha's warm invitation, Mary might not have had the opportunity to sit at Jesus' feet and listen to his words. We need to take advantage of opportunities and circumstances so that we can listen to God. Do you seize times to hear and learn more from the Lord as Mary did? She recognised the value of this time, sitting at Jesus' feet and listening attentively. She dared not miss any of Jesus' valuable teaching. Do you take the opportunity every day to listen to God?

Don't be distracted (vs 40–42)

Martha simply wished to welcome Jesus in her home by preparing a good meal. Her motives were good, but her priorities were mixed up. What was most important was listening to Jesus. He might not ever be in their home again – he certainly would not be available to them much longer. It was a chance not to be missed; but Martha was missing that chance because she was distracted by other matters. It is easy to be distracted. Daily responsibilities and cares take away from our most important priorities. It is easy to spend the days neglecting our time with God. However, it is necessary to stop and consider the most important things in life and give them our first priority. Jesus allowed Mary to stay by his side, for she chose the most valuable thing for herself. What are your top priorities in life?

Prayer: Lord, enable me to discern what is valuable in life in order to keep my priorities straight. Draw me closer, to have private moments with you each day.

Teach us to pray

If you ask, God will answer you.

LUKE 11:1–13

Main verse: 'So I say to you: Ask and it will be given to you; seek and you will find; knock and the door will be opened to you.'

Pray to your Father (vs 1–4)
The key elements of prayer are included in the simple prayer Jesus taught his disciples (vs 2-4). Prayer must include an element of praise. We should enter into God's presence acknowledging who he is (v 2). People of faith also express in their prayers a belief in God's promises. Therefore, Jesus taught his disciples to pray for God's kingdom which was to come. Another essential element of prayer is confession of sin (v 4). There cannot be genuine communion with God while there is still some unconfessed sin in our lives. Finally, we bring our needs to God. Although he is aware of them, he wants us to express our trust in him. Which of these basic elements do you neglect when you pray? How can you begin practising a more balanced prayer life?

Ask and you will receive (vs 5–13)
One of the reasons we don't receive answers to our prayers is simply because we do not ask. Jesus encourages us to be bold (v 9). Our friends may be reluctant to assist us, but God is different. No request is too big or too small for his consideration. Jesus also gives us an affirmation that God keeps his promises (v 13). Believe in the promises of God as you pray – he promises to give us what we ask. Our loving heavenly Father will give what is best for us, not what will harm us. Therefore, not receiving what you've asked for does not mean God has broken his promise, but that he considered it harmful for you. What do you need to ask for? Do you believe in his promise?

Prayer: Father, help me to believe that you are more ready to answer than I am to ask, and so to be bold in my praying.

Jesus – stronger than Satan

Learn to trust in the superior power of Jesus.

LUKE 11:14–28

Main verse: 'But if I drive out demons by the finger of God, then the kingdom of God has come to you.'

Believe in the power of Jesus (vs 14–20)

Some chose to believe that Jesus drove out demons by the power of Satan rather than by his own power. There are other people who will not believe in the evidence presented before their eyes. Because they are not satisfied with what they see, they are led to seek more proof. Jesus posed challenges for each group. To the first group, he exposed their illogical reasoning – why would Satan drive out Satan? To the second group he challenged their unbelief. Without demonstrating their own power to cast out demons, they continually expressed unbelief. These verses prompt us to examine our blind tendency toward cynical scepticism. Do you believe in the power of God?

Fill your heart with his Word (vs 21–28)

Each time Jesus drove out an evil spirit, he demonstrated his superior power over Satan. It was logical. Why would the evil spirit choose to leave someone whom he had long possessed, unless a stronger person had come and driven him out? Jesus gives some serious warnings to us. He reminds us that it is not enough to have the influence of sin and evil driven from our lives, but that we must allow God to fill the empty space with his Spirit. His final word commands us to commit our lives in obedience to the Word of God in order to be free from the power of evil. Are you empowered by the Word of God each day? Are you Spirit-filled?

Prayer: Mighty Lord, I praise you because no one is more powerful than you. Help me to trust in this power.

What are you looking for?

Seeing is not necessarily believing, but believing is seeing.

LUKE 11:29-36

Main verse: 'Your eye is the lamp of your body. When your eyes are good, your whole body also is full of light. But when they are bad, your body also is full of darkness.'

Learn to live by faith (vs 29–32)

In Jesus' day, people requested him to perform miracles. In reality, they were seeking supernatural power to base their faith on. But, in fact, they had no intention of believing. People see only what they want to see. They were simply seeking something sensational. Jesus refused to submit to their wishes. Signs and wonders will convince no one of the reality of Christ if there is no desire to seek him through repentance. Is the truth of a resurrected Christ enough to draw you to faith? Is your faith resting on visible evidences, or on the transforming Word of God?

Discern what you see (vs 33–36)

God's Word was made to shine into our hearts, to expose the darkness and sin within. But some prefer to go on living in sin and darkness; they keep the light of God's Word hidden. Jesus warns us to be discerning about what we allow our eyes to see. What we allow our eyes to see will feed our hearts. If we choose to spend our time looking at evil things, then our minds become increasingly filled with evil thoughts which in turn influence us to commit evil deeds. On the other hand, if we open our hearts to the light of God's Word, his Spirit will expose and remove our sin from us and fill our hearts with truth. Where are your eyes directed? How do you decide what you expose your eyes to?

Prayer: Today, O Lord, help me to focus on what is good and pure, true and beautiful, right and admirable.

Don't be a hypocrite

God's Word wants to expose your sin and set you free from it.

LUKE 11:37-54

Main verse: 'Woe to you experts in the law, because you have taken away the key to knowledge. You yourselves have not entered, and you have hindered those who were entering.'

Let God's Word penetrate your heart (vs 37–44)

According to the Pharisees, sin was always directly associated with behaviour. If you kept certain rules, you could consider yourself free from sin. If, on the other hand, you broke those rules, clearly you were a sinner. They overlooked a very important and fundamental aspect of God's teaching – that the influence of sin goes deeper than just outward behaviour. Sin permeates one's heart and mind. So Jesus challenged the Pharisees about their hypocrisy. More important than actions are the motives behind them. A gift generously given to God loses its value if only the giver receives the adulation. Do you examine motives for your actions? How are you affected by people's responses?

Choose the living Word (vs 45–54)

In our ignorance and misunderstanding, we can render the gospel ineffective. If Christians are primarily concerned with a list of dos and don'ts, we have missed the essence of the gospel. The gospel is not a 'gospel of doing' – it is a gospel of grace and faith. Jesus came to set us free from a 'gospel of doing'. We are also guilty of exterminating the living Word of God. Prophets came and were killed for speaking the living and true Word of God. God's living Word causes discomfort to people because it is like a two-edged sword. Have you chosen and practised the Word of God to make you an effective witness for Jesus? How do you understand the essence of the gospel? Does this gospel challenge your thoughts and actions?

Prayer: Father, I want your word to sift my heart, to search my motives and to govern my life today.

Don't be afraid

God is the one to be ultimately feared.

LUKE 12:1–12

Main verse: 'But I will show you whom you should fear: Fear him who, after the killing of the body, has power to throw you into hell. Yes, I tell you, fear him.'

Fear God only (vs 1–5)
God knows our words and actions. He knows our thoughts and motives. Many people commit sins in secret – no one knows about them but God. God hates hypocrisy, and sometimes the only way he is able to deal with the problem is to expose those private sins (vs 2,3). Once it is out in the open, God gives us an opportunity for repentance. We are to fear this God who knows everything about us. If we fear only him, our fears about others will be under his control. Other people may hurt us in this life, but God knows and cares. Trusting in his power enables us to be assured of his protection. What private sins have you been involved in? Will today be your opportunity to repent and turn away?

Don't fear anything else (vs 6–12)
Jesus reminds us that God knows our needs individually and meets them because he really cares for us. We don't need to be afraid. Some people are afraid that they will not have enough to eat or drink. Others may fear that God will reject them on the last day. If you neglect God and refuse to acknowledge him before people, you have reasons to be afraid; but if you gladly testify of your Lord before people, be secure (vs 8,9): Jesus said that he will gladly testify of you before his Father in heaven. Some people are afraid of persecution, but Jesus promises that they can be bold through the Holy Spirit's power. What prevents you from acknowledging Jesus before your friends and family? How is fear related to your lack of faith?

Prayer: Lord, I'm so sensitive to other's opinions, when you are the one I should fear and acknowledge. Help me to change.

71

Where are your riches?

Are your riches in heaven or on earth?

LUKE 12:13–21

Main verse: 'Then he said to them, "Watch out! Be on your guard against all kinds of greed; a man's life does not consist in the abundance of his possessions."'

There is more to life than money (vs 13–15)

Jesus was teaching important spiritual truths to people, but one man's focus was on something else. His mind was taken up solely with his earthly possessions. He wanted Jesus to be the arbiter in a dispute he was having with his brother over their inheritance (v 13). Becoming enslaved by greed blinds our minds to spiritual things. Jesus warns elsewhere that you cannot love God and money at the same time (16:13). Of course, greed for money is not the only form of greed which can have this effect. Greed for power, position, fame or praise creates conflict between God and us. What do you seek from God? How valuable are material things to you? What particular form of greed are you most vulnerable to?

Being rich towards God (vs 16–21)

Jesus tells us the story of a man who was totally absorbed in himself and in his material possessions. He was the kind of person who was only interested in himself and talked only about himself. He talked about what he had accomplished – about what he possessed and his future plans (vs 18,19). Not for one minute did he have a thought for anyone else; nor do we see his thoughts directed toward God. He never thought of death or eternity because he was only concerned with his life on earth. He didn't consider that with death one loses all possessions and must answer to God (v 20). This story teaches us to store up riches in heaven through our life of faith and obedience to God. What kind of treasures have you stored up in heaven? Do they outweigh your earthly riches?

Prayer: Father help me not to fool myself. Please show me, am I storing up my riches in heaven or on earth?

Don't worry

With right priorities you can rest in peace.

LUKE 12:22–34

Main verse: 'But seek his kingdom, and these things will be given to you as well.'

Worrying is a waste of time (vs 22–26)

Jesus wants our lives to be free from worry. He offers us sound and sensible words on living a worry-free life. First, he reminds us that there are more important things in life than food and clothes (v 23). Food and clothing are necessary, but we are to be concerned about more valuable things. Second, we need to remember that God is in control (v 24). He knows our needs – he loves us and will supply these things. If he does it for the birds of the air; how much more will he do it for human beings (v 24). Finally, he tells us that worrying is a waste of time. No amount of worrying helps us solve problems; in fact, worrying only hinders us from finding the solutions to our problems. Take your worries to God and trust in him. Have you been needlessly worrying about something?

Get your priorities right (vs 27–34)

Jesus continually deals with the problem of worry in our lives. He encourages us to believe (v 28). We are to trust God to supply all our needs. Trusting in God relieves our worry. If God can perform such a splendid job of clothing the flowers, he can do even more for you. He reminds us that we should be different from unbelievers who spend their time worrying about trivial things. He admonishes us to get our priorities straight. If we concentrate on what God has given us to do, he will certainly take care of our daily needs. Finally, he advises us to live for eternal matters. We must be free from our attachment to material things. What do you live for? Write out your life's priorities in order.

Prayer: Lord, help me to put your work first, not to worry, and to trust you to take care of my needs.

Always be ready

Are you prepared for Jesus' return?

LUKE 12:35–48

Main verse: 'You also must be ready, because the Son of Man will come at an hour when you do not expect him.'

Keep your lamps burning (vs 35–40)

Jesus promised to return, yet no one knows exactly when he will come again. He expects his people to be ready and waiting with expectant hearts (vs 35,36). He doesn't want us to be asleep; he wants the lights to be shining. Just as a thief comes at night when we least expect him, so Jesus may also come at the most unexpected time. For those who are ready there will be a great reward. Being delighted by their faithfulness, Jesus will acknowledge their sincere faith. The humility and grace of the Lord Jesus Christ is immeasurable. If Jesus were to come today, would you be ready? Are there still some things you need to change? How can you best prepare yourself?

Fulfil your responsibility (vs 41–48)

When Jesus gives us a responsibility, he expects us to fulfil it. There are people who waste much time before carrying out God-given tasks. They are lazy with their responsibilities. They fail to realise that other people are inconvenienced by their delay and, most of all, that God is displeased by their delayed obedience. Then there are others who may accept responsibilities from God, but seize their opportunity to abuse the authority given them. Certainly, there is great joy and fulfilment in accepting a responsibility from God, while there is punishment for those who neglect their task. Jesus will be greatly pleased with those people who are faithful and diligent in their work. What responsibilities have you received from God? Are you faithfully fulfilling them?

Prayer: Convince me of the reality of your return, Lord, so that I live every day in expectation of it.

The cost of peace

The price of peace involves great suffering.

LUKE 12:49-59

Main verse: 'I have come to bring fire on the earth, and how I wish it were already kindled!'

Expect division in your family (vs 49–53)

Accomplishing salvation for men and women was costly for Jesus. It caused great physical, mental and spiritual suffering. However, Jesus looked forward to establishing peace between God and human beings and willingly endured the suffering. Yet, on the other hand, his gospel would result in division and disruption to many families, as one member of a family accepts Jesus while another rejects him. People who choose to believe must count the cost of following Jesus. This may entail choosing between family and Jesus Christ. Have you encountered the high cost of following Jesus? What choices have you made recently that cost you highly?

Make peace with your neighbour (vs 54–59)

Jesus raised two different issues here for us to consider. First, he charged how quickly people showed expertise at interpreting signs for the weather but failed to understand and interpret the spiritual climate (vs 54–56). This issue is related to a matter of priorities. Jesus was probing about which issue possessed deeper significance – whether it would rain tomorrow or that God would come to his people? We need God's help to understand the spiritual signs of our times. The second issue is a simple and practical one. If you have a dispute with a neighbour, attempt to solve the problem between yourselves. Through this, Christian principles can be applied; but handing the conflict over to the court leaves your dispute at the mercy of a secular legal system. Are you facing problems with someone? How can you best resolve it?

Prayer: Lord Jesus, when following you brings hardship, may the way you willingly endured suffering inspire me to keep going.

Bear fruit for God

Personal repentance must come before judging others.

LUKE 13:1–9

Main verse: 'I tell you, no! But unless you repent, you too will all perish.'

Repent (vs 1–5)

It is very tempting to accuse people of being involved in sin when misfortune befalls them. We easily become engrossed in judging other people's sins. Undoubtedly it is easier to see the sins of other people than our own. However, the same judgement that awaits them for their sin awaits us for our own sins. There is only one solution to sins we commit and that is through repentance. Therefore, before self-righteously passing judgement on the sins of others, we must fully repent of our own (vs 3,5). We need the Spirit's help both in acknowledgement and repentance of sin. Are you quick to judge the flaws of others? Have you repented of your own sins?

Bear fruit for God (vs 6–9)

Jesus saved us so that in due time we would bear fruit. Of course, the fruits of our salvation might not be visible immediately but must be manifested at some point. There should be the fruit of changed lives. He desires to see our characters becoming more like him each day. He expects that others will come to know him through our life's witness. Jesus waits and gives us encouragement to bear these fruits. But if some of us do not bear fruit to the end, there wasn't a real transformation in our hearts from the start. Are you bearing fruit for Jesus? How are your fruits manifested?

Prayer: Father, forgive my haste in condemning others, my blindness to my own faults and my fruitlessness. Help me to change.

Freedom in Jesus

Jesus frees us from Satan and other forms of evil.

LUKE 13:10–21

Main verse: 'When Jesus saw her, he called her forward and said to her, "Woman, you are set free from your infirmity."'

Pray to be set free (vs 10–17)

Undoubtedly, some problems we face are a direct result of Satan's involvement in our lives. In the case of certain sickness, people's need was not so much to be healed physically as to be set free from Satan's control. We notice Jesus healed people's diseases in some instances, while in others he dealt with the influence of Satan. We should ask the Lord to discern the real nature of their problems and struggles. The woman in this passage had been bound by Satan for eighteen years (v 11). Today, Jesus' power can set us free from our diseases and from Satan's bondage. However, narrow-mindedness, hypocrisy and legalism seriously limits believers from experiencing God's healing work in people's lives. To what extent has legalism affected your thoughts and emotions? Does it limit your love for others?

Pray for the kingdom of God (vs 18–21)

Expanding God's kingdom involves his freedom to take something small and weak to begin a great work. For example, a mustard seed is able to grow into a tree big enough to provide shelter for birds (v 19). Also, a little bit of yeast makes the dough become big enough to feed many people. Don't ever think that anything you have to offer God is too small for him to use. Your money, time or talent can be used greatly if entrusted into God's hands. The kingdom of God will be established in our nation by humble people offering their best to God. Every little thing that you withhold from God is one less thing God can use to expand his work. What is your 'mustard seed' that you can offer to God today?

Prayer: Take my life, Lord; it's not very much, but it's all I've got. Take it and multiply it like a mustard seed.

Jesus – the way of salvation

Jesus is the only way you can approach God.

LUKE 13:22–35

Main verse: 'O Jerusalem, Jerusalem, you who kill the prophets and stone those sent to you, how often I have longed to gather your children together, as a hen gathers her chicks under her wings, but you were not willing!'

Enter by the narrow gate (vs 22–30)

Many people will wait until it is too late to make their peace with Jesus. The way of salvation is indeed narrow. It is only through commitment to Christ that a person can be saved. Casual acknowledgement and vague commitment to Jesus will not be sufficient on the day of judgement. We must be fully committed to Jesus Christ now. Full commitment involves a real personal relationship with him. Only then can we look forward to being welcomed to enjoy the kingdom of God. What does it mean to know and have a personal relationship with him? Do these words encourage you to make a serious commitment to Jesus?

Come to Jesus (vs 31–35)

Despite Jesus' clear warnings, many people rejected him. The Pharisees tried to get rid of him on the pretext that Herod wanted to kill him (v 31). Jesus, however, was secure in the will of his Father (v 32). He knew that he had to die in Jerusalem. He knew that no king, however powerful, could thwart God's timing. His death and resurrection would be according to God's time. Rejection by the Pharisees and the people of Jerusalem did not stop Jesus from reaching out in one last loving appeal to the people (vs 34,35). His fervent desire to draw people unto himself still continues. It is up to them to respond. We must share Jesus' love with them, while letting them know the consequences of rejecting Jesus. Is your heart eager to reach out to unbelievers? Does your love for Jesus move you to love them?

Prayer: Lord Jesus, I'm continually stunned by your love for people. Enable me to love others in this way.

Living in his likeness

Strive for holiness in every aspect of your life.

LUKE 14:1–14

Main verse: 'For everyone who exalts himself will be humbled, and he who humbles himself will be exalted.'

Be compassionate (vs 1–6)

God's law reveals his nature. However, the Pharisees so distorted the law through their own misinterpretations, rules and regulations that they presented a very different message and understanding of God to the people. The Pharisees succeeded in portraying a harsh, intolerant and uncompassionate God. Jesus challenged this notion when he healed a man on the Sabbath day (v 4). Through it, people began to see a loving and compassionate God. This poses a serious question for us to answer. By our traditions and way of life, what kind of God do we present before men? Do you show God's compassion or your own lack of love?

Be humble (vs 7–14)

One of the ways we can convey to people God's nature and work in our lives is through our humility. Few will be attracted to a God whose people are self-centred and self-seeking. Few people will be attracted to those who constantly exalt themselves over others. Few people will be attracted to a God whose people only do good with an eye to the reward they will receive. By contrast, a loving and humble spirit will draw many people to an ever more loving and generous God. Again we need to ask ourselves, when people look at us, what kind of God do they see? What characteristics of God do you reflect in your life?

Prayer: Father, may my life be marked by compassion and humility so that others realise you are a loving and generous God.

Come to Jesus

Jesus eagerly and patiently waits for you.

LUKE 14:15–24

Main verse: 'Then the master told his servant, "Go out to the roads and country lanes and make them come in, so that my house will be full."'

Don't make excuses (vs 15–20)

No one will have an acceptable excuse for not responding to the call of the gospel. In this story the man had already invited all his guests (v 16). They knew when the banquet was to be held. They could have easily set aside time for this occasion, yet they made weak excuses not to come. Also it is clear that everything had already been prepared by the servants (v 17). Guests needed only to respond to the invitation and attend the feast. Likewise, it is the glorious truth of the gospel that Jesus has already done everything necessary on the cross for our salvation. All that is left for us to do is to come and receive him into our hearts. What excuses have prevented you from committing yourself to God? Give thanks for God's persistence.

Invite people to come (vs 21–24)

God's plans will not be thwarted. When the Jewish people refused the invitation to come to Jesus, God simply offered the gospel to the Gentile people. It didn't matter to him that they were poor, crippled, blind or lame – he was glad to welcome them into his kingdom (v 21). No one is too unworthy to be accepted by God. God joyfully accepts you just as you are; he makes the changes. As expected, some people need a measure of persuasion before they will come to Jesus. Although you cannot force anyone to believe, you can make efforts to share with them the truth of God's Word. Is there someone you are compelled to share the gospel with? As you pray, trust that God will give you the opportunity and the boldness to share.

Prayer: Father, show me how pathetic my excuses are which are holding me back from following you.

Count the cost

Being a Christian can be costly.

LUKE 14:25-35

Main verse: 'And anyone who does not carry his cross and follow me cannot be my disciple.'

Take up your cross (vs 25–30)

Jesus never promised that being a Christian would be easy. Before anyone becomes his follower, Jesus wants them to count the cost. For some people the cost may involve giving up other responsibilities. For others, it may mean a breach in family relationships (v 26). For some chosen ones, it may entail leaving their family to go abroad to share the gospel. The fundamental question is whether or not we are committed to love Jesus and obey his will. Are you? Every Christian is called to carry his cross and follow Jesus. Every true disciple of Christ must be willing to suffer for him even to the point of death. Are you willing? Count the cost before you decide to follow Jesus. How far will you go to follow Jesus?

Living for Jesus (vs 31–35)

Jesus' calling of men and women prepares them to be transforming instruments in the world. He wants his people to be salt in this world. Salt functions to preserve what is good, and we must be devoted at preserving all that is good and pure in our society. Salt also functions to give flavour. Christians should demonstrate clearly the best kind of lifestyle. In order to carry out these two vital functions, Christians must become actively involved in society. We must be willing to give up our own self-interests to that end, and also preserve our distinctiveness. As a Christian, are you perceived to be different and unique? What are you doing to improve your society?

Prayer: Thank you, Jesus, for stating so clearly the cost of being a disciple. Help me to take up my cross and follow you.

Lost and found

Jesus seeks to find and gather all his people.

LUKE 15:1–10

Main verse: 'I tell you that in the same way there is more rejoicing in heaven over one sinner who repents than over ninety-nine righteous persons who do not need to repent.'

Jesus loves you (vs 1–7)

The Pharisees could not understand why Jesus spent so much time with 'sinners' and outcasts. But, in Jesus' eyes they were the people who most desperately needed him. He would find them and bring them home. The story of the lost sheep illustrates that each individual person is of tremendous importance to Jesus. Jesus yearns for that one lost person. He is concerned about each one of his people even in the midst of a crowd. People may wander away from him, but his love will seek them out. Furthermore, our Lord rejoices greatly each time one of the lost repents and comes to him. Truly you are precious to Jesus. Do you view and treat each person with respect? Pray for a heart of compassion toward the lost.

Jesus will not give up on us (vs 8–10)

The second parable illustrates the efforts that Jesus will take to find those who are lost. The woman lost a coin. She still had nine left, but she intently searched until she found the coin. She lit a lamp and carefully swept every corner of her house. Likewise, Jesus will not give up until he has found all those who are his. That lost coin may seem small and insignificant, but to her its value caused her to tell her neighbours and rejoice with them (v 9). Every time a sinner repents, regardless of their status, we can imagine Jesus rushing around to share this great news to heavenly angels. Are you concerned about the salvation of someone you love? Have you experienced reasons to give up on that person? Consider the woman who lost the coin.

Prayer: Jesus, thank you that you came to seek and to save the lost. Create in me the desire to do this too.

The prodigal son

With open arms, God waits even when we go astray.

LUKE 15:11-24

Main verse: '"For this son of mine was dead and is alive again; he was lost and is found." So they began to celebrate.'

A wayward son (vs 11–20a)
Most young people are eager to get on with their own lives. They are usually confident that they are prepared for independence and that they know better than anyone else. The young man in this story wanted to enjoy life while he was young. Although he wanted to experience life in its fullness, he experienced emptiness instead because he placed his hopes on money and pleasure. Wealth seems to offer much pleasure and fulfilment, but what it usually delivers is emptiness and degradation. Fortunately, the young man eventually realised his mistake and went back to his father. Real freedom and enjoyment can only be found in a relationship with God - a relationship of father and son. Have you sometimes been tempted to sacrifice your relationship with the Lord for the empty promises of the world? How do you deal with such temptations?

A loving father (vs 20b–24)
What a marvellous picture we see of God the Father in these verses! First, God allows us freedom to make decisions and learn from our own experiences. Through this story of the father and son we see God watching and waiting for the first glimpse of our desire to return to him. The moment God senses our desire for repentance, he rushes toward us, arms outstretched to embrace, welcome and restore his children. The moment the words of repentance are uttered, forgiveness is granted; all past sins are wiped out of the Father's mind and he celebrates the restoration of the child. Do you doubt God's infinite mercy? Remember, he always welcomes your return with open arms.

Prayer: Lord God, you made us for yourself and our hearts are restless until they find rest in you (Augustine).

The elder brother

By requesting, you will receive.

Luke 15:25-32

Main verse: '"My son," the father said, "you are always with me, and everything I have is yours."'

Avoid bitterness (vs 25–30)

For years the older brother played the role of the faithful son. He had stayed at home with his father, working faithfully for him. Even when his brother came home, he was out labouring in the fields. In a way, he had a right to be resentful that no one had summoned him home from the fields to join the party for his brother's return. But his angry reaction revealed a much deeper problem. For years he had been nursing a bitter resentment in his heart (vs 29,30). He was bitter at his younger brother who seemed to get everything he wanted. He was bitter at his father for overlooking his needs. He felt cheated. Bitterness kills joy in our hearts and corrodes our relationships. Bitterness robs joy from our service and causes us to serve simply out of duty, not love. Is there bitterness at the root of your unhappiness?

Rejoice (vs 31,32)

Just as the father had gone out to meet the returning prodigal, again he went out to meet the resentful older son. God is in the business of reconciliation and it is he who comes all the way to meet us. Here, the older son forgot that he was the son of his father and began to think of himself as a servant. Serving God out of duty and not out of love changes your perspective and kills the joy of service. He also forgot that as a son, everything that his father owned was his and was available to him. All he needed to do was ask. Finally, he forgot that the prodigal was his brother. Any brother who returns should be welcomed home. Do you sometimes forget to ask God for what you need? Do you rejoice in your brothers and sisters in Christ?

Prayer: Father, I confess the grudging and bitter spirit with which I sometimes serve. Remind me that I am your child and your heir.

Use your money wisely

Is money your master, or is God?

LUKE 16:1–15

Main verse: 'No servant can serve two masters. Either he will hate the one and love the other, or he will be devoted to the one and despise the other. You cannot serve both God and money.'

Be wise (vs 1–8)

The manager in this story must be condemned for his dishonesty. He had already misused his master's possessions and in order to solve his dilemma, he misused them again. But while he cannot be commended for his dishonesty, he can be commended for his shrewdness. When he was faced with a problem, he faced up to it squarely and considered the possible alternatives. When faced with a problem, many Christians prolong their situation rather than deal with it directly. The manager thought about his problem, made a clear decision about how he would handle it and took action. He won many friends for himself, and even his master approved of his shrewdness (v 8). What problem in your life do you need to face up to squarely and take positive action to solve?

Be trustworthy (vs 9–15)

Jesus teaches us to use material possessions responsibly and wisely. Our attitude toward material wealth has spiritual consequences (v 9). Jesus says that we should use our wealth for good, to benefit friends and nurture fellowship. Use your wealth for others and blessings will follow. Also, when we prove ourselves trustworthy with the use of our money, God entrusts us with spiritual wealth. People who abuse material responsibility must not be in charge of spiritual responsibility. Furthermore, a person should have clear priorities. He cannot make both money and God a top priority (v 13). We need to choose which we place as our first commitment. Can you be trusted to use money wisely? Honestly, which do you serve more – God or money?

Prayer: Help me, Lord, to be both wise and trustworthy as I handle my possessions, and always to make you my true master.

Repent and believe!

Where will you spend your eternity?

LUKE 16:16–31

Main verse: 'He said to him, "If they do not listen to Moses and the Prophets, they will not be convinced even if someone rises from the dead."'

Believe the gospel (vs 16–18)

Until John the Baptist came, the only gospel people had was found in the Old Testament. The Old Testament message is the same as the New Testament message as proclaimed by John the Baptist, Jesus and Paul. The message has never changed; it has just become easier to understand. The final conclusion of the parable of the rich man and Lazarus (v 31) is that the way of salvation has been promised in the Old Testament. God has not changed his message. There are certain truths which are eternal. For example, God's attitude toward divorce will not change simply because the attitudes of society do (v 18). All that we need to know to follow God is contained in the Bible. Our life depends on what we do with the gospel. Do you accept the whole Word of God?

Decide now! (vs 19–31)

This story clearly illustrates a direct connection between our present response to the gospel and our eternal destiny. The rich man knew well that the reason he was suffering in hell was not because he was rich, but because he refused to believe in the gospel and repent. Equally, by implication, the reason Lazarus was in heaven was not because of his suffering and poverty, but because he repented and believed the gospel. Two lessons stand out clearly in this parable. First of all, our eternal fate will be determined now in this life according to what we do with the gospel. After death, that fate cannot be changed (vs 25,26). Secondly, if people do not accept and believe in the gospel by the truth itself, nothing will convince them, including miracles.

Prayer: Father, I confess with my lips, 'Jesus is Lord', and believe in my heart that you raised him from the dead.

Faith – forgiveness – faithfulness

Real faith expresses itself in a forgiving spirit and faithful service.

LUKE 17:1–10

Main verse: 'He replied, "If you have faith as small as a mustard seed, you can say to this mulberry tree, 'Be uprooted and planted in the sea,' and it will obey you."'

Be forgiving (vs 1–4)

Christians are responsible for one another. We must not underestimate the power of sin. Because Jesus knew that sin would be a constant problem for us, he instructs us not to cause other people to sin. The careless behaviour of one Christian can easily draw others into sin. A bad example by a Christian leader can cause many to stumble and fall. Furthermore, Jesus tells us that we are to rebuke one another for sin (v 3). Many Christians remain indifferent to their brothers and sisters. When someone sins, we are quick to gossip or overlook the sin rather than admonish the person regarding it. Finally, Jesus teaches us to be forgiving (vs 3,4). Because he has forgiven us much, we must also forgive one another much. Is there anything in your life which might cause others to stumble? Have you been forgiving to your brothers and sisters in Christ?

Be faithful (vs 5–10)

Jesus wants to correct two mistaken attitudes. First, many people, like the disciples, seem to think that stronger faith can accomplish more for God. But Jesus says that even the smallest amount of faith has the power to do great things for God (v 6). He emphasises the sincerity of our faith, not the amount of faith. Secondly, Jesus corrects our mistaken attitude of wanting to be praised and rewarded for our service to God. We are servants of God. He owes us nothing. On the contrary, it is we who should offer our faithful service to God as a result of our faith in Christ. Any reward or blessing he bestows on us is based on his grace, not our merit. Does your faith in Jesus inspire greater faithfulness in your life?

Prayer: Lord, help my faith to be sincere and my service to be gladly given.

Be thankful

As you receive from God, learn to give him the praise and glory.

LUKE 17:11–19

Main verse: 'He threw himself at Jesus' feet and thanked him – and he was a Samaritan.'

Seize your chance
(vs 11–14)

Ten men were united in a common problem – each had leprosy. Sharing in a common plight tends to bring people together. The ten leprosy sufferers did three rightful things. First, they seized an important opportunity. They respectfully kept their distance from Jesus, but allowed their cries to be heard by him (v 13). Next they threw themselves at his mercy. They pleaded with him to have compassion on them. Finally, they obeyed his command. On their way to the priest they were healed (v 14). Seize the opportunity to cast your troubles on Jesus, and his grace will meet your needs. Have you neglected to do any of these things in looking for the solution you need?

Give God the glory
(vs 15–19)

While the ten leprosy sufferers should be commended for their belief, nine of them forgot one important thing. They forgot to return to give thanks to Jesus and praise God. Perhaps the other nine leprosy sufferers thought God was obligated to heal them? The Samaritan leprosy sufferer thought otherwise. He acknowledged what God had done for him; and henceforth, he honoured and praised God for his mercy (vs 15,16). Thanking God pleases him, and offering praise to God will bring recognition from him. So the Samaritan leprosy sufferer received high commendation from Jesus. Besides being physically healed, the leprosy sufferer experienced mental and spiritual wholeness as well. Living as an outcast for years must have left its painful scar on his character, but now Jesus completely healed him. Is there something you have forgotten to give thanks for? Give God your thanks today.

Prayer: With all my heart I praise the Lord! I will never forget how kind he has been.

The kingdom of God

Does Jesus reign in your heart?

LUKE 17:20–37

Main verse: 'For the Son of Man in his day will be like the lightning, which flashes and lights up the sky from one end to the other.'

The kingdom is within you (vs 20–25)

The kingdom of God is not an easy concept to understand. God promised that his kingdom, which is unlike any worldly kingdom, would come. Therefore we cannot look for the kingdom in worldly terms. Jesus tells us that his kingdom is a spiritual kingdom which begins in the hearts of some people (v 21). When Jesus is invited into one's heart, his kingdom begins to rule within them, residing there silently. But there will come a day when the kingdom of God will be audible and visible (v 24). On this day, Jesus will not come secretly. Instead, the presence of Jesus will be so real that no one can doubt he is Lord. Is Jesus reigning in your life? Has his kingdom been established in your heart?

The kingdom will come (vs 26–37)

The world will probably be insensitive to the imminence of Jesus' Second Coming. Many people will be indifferent to the end of the world and the coming day of judgement. There will be two distinct groups – those who believed in Jesus and those who did not. Jesus will gather all those who are his, but those who lived their lives without Christ will be rejected. They will lose everything. Being related to a believer will not win a person into the kingdom, only a close relationship with Jesus will. No one knows of Jesus' return, therefore we must live as though he may come tomorrow. Many people still lead lives without God. How can you help? Are you living a meaningful life in Christ, knowing he may come soon?

Prayer: Father, your kingdom come, your will be done, in my life today, as it is in heaven.

Keep on praying

God longs to answer your persistent prayers.

Luke 18:1–8

Main verse: 'And will not God bring about justice for his chosen ones, who cry out to him day and night? Will he keep putting them off?'

The unjust judge (vs 1–5)

The widow in this story faced many odds against her. First, as a widow, she had no one to defend her. She was alone with little influence because she had lost her husband. Secondly, someone had taken advantage of her situation. Thirdly, the judge who could help her was a man with no conscience. He did not fear God and lacked natural compassion which she hoped to arouse (v 2). Her only weapon was persistence. She did not give up. Eventually she succeeded in getting what she wanted, not because she aroused in him a sense of justice or compassion but because of her persistent efforts. Do you recall times when your persistence in prayer was rewarded and answered?

The God of justice (vs 6–8)

By comparison, most of us suffer fewer disadvantages than the widow. But like her, we have adversaries who will seek to take advantage of us. Yet we have Jesus – our advocate – to argue our case. We have the One whose justice serves those who suffer unjustly. Our God is compassionate, and lovingly aids his own children. This moves us to persist in our prayers until God responds. Often we experience God's answers quickly, but at other times we are called to exercise our faith by persevering. Can God find this kind of persistence in you? Have you ever cried out to him 'day and night'? Do you trust that our merciful God will not put aside your cries to him?

Prayer: Lord, teach me to pray as Jacob did: 'I will not let you go unless you bless me'.

Pray humbly

Humble yourself and you will be exalted.

LUKE 18:9-17

Main verse: 'I tell you that this man, rather than the other, went home justified before God. For everyone who exalts himself will be humbled, and he who humbles himself will be exalted.'

Humble yourself before God (vs 9–14)

The Pharisee was ignorant of his sins. He boasted of all the good deeds he had done. He talked of nothing but himself. Yet he keenly recognised the sins of others. Though he appeared to be praying to God, he was in fact exhibiting false piety before people. The actions of the Pharisee are often the very ones we are guilty of. The tax collector also prayed about himself, but in a different way. He sincerely desired to confess his sins and to receive forgiveness from God. He did not rely on his good works but on the mercy of God. He humbled himself before God, and his humility serves as a model for us to follow. God desires a humble attitude more than outward appearance. Is there some sin you need to confess before God?

Become as a little child (vs 15–17)

Here the disciples tried to protect Jesus by forbidding children to approach him. But they failed to understand his character. Jesus doesn't refuse anyone who wants to come to him. Jesus willingly spares time for those who need him. Perhaps the disciples mistakenly considered some people to be more important than others and thought Jesus shouldn't be bothered with children. Such a misunderstanding was responsible for keeping some people from coming to Jesus. Have some of your attitudes kept people from believing in God? Jesus' response is to encourage us to become like trusting, innocent children. Will you take time to evaluate your heart?

Prayer: Lord Jesus Christ, Son of the living God, have mercy on me, for I am a sinner.

How can I receive eternal life?

Only Jesus has the power to save us and give us life.

LUKE 18:18–30

Main verse: 'When Jesus heard this, he said to him, "You still lack one thing. Sell everything you have and give to the poor, and you will have treasure in heaven. Then come, follow me."'

Put God first in your life (vs 18–23)

When the ruler asked this important question of obtaining eternal life, he assumed that the solution was simply a matter of keeping God's law. Outwardly he followed this command well, and yet there was a lack of assurance in his heart. When a person tries to save himself by his own efforts, uncertainty and doubt linger. Such people continually question the sufficiency of their labour. But the essence of this matter is not what we do, but how we relate to God. Jesus exposes the man's lack of intimate relationship with God by asking him to give up what is most valuable to him, namely his material possessions (v 22). This does not imply that sacrificing your possessions saves you. Rather, salvation comes by putting God first in your life. Is God first in your life? How is it reflected?

Trust God for the impossible (vs 24–30)

Many believed that the rich were especially blessed by God. So they were surprised when Jesus said that it is hard for the rich to be saved (vs 24,25). It is hard for the rich to be saved because their riches easily and often become a substitute for God in their lives. Also, regardless of whether one is rich or poor, no one can save themselves and take away their own sins. However, Jesus said, 'what is impossible with men is possible with God' (v 27). We must trust God, since he alone can save us. Following God means being willing to forsake everything for him. Doing so ensures God's blessings of eternal life. Are you fully trusting in the God of the impossible for your salvation?

Prayer: Father, I want to hold onto things so much. Help me to let go of them and give myself over entirely to you.

What do you want from Jesus?

Only the Lord can help us understand and see his Word.

LUKE 18:31-43

Main verse: 'Immediately he received his sight and followed Jesus, praising God. When all the people saw it, they also praised God.'

We need understanding (vs 31–34)

Jesus repeatedly told his disciples that he would soon have to go to Jerusalem and die there; but that after three days he would rise again from the dead (vs 31-33). Yet this revelation they could not grasp (v 34). Probably, part of the problem was that they did not want to understand. They did not want to face the truth that Jesus was going to die soon. Also their thoughts could have been influenced by Satan, who strives to confuse our minds to misunderstand the truths of the gospel. But verse 34 reveals another reason for their lack of understanding. It simply was not time for them to comprehend this mystery in God's plan. Do you pray that God will lead you into a better understanding of his Word?

We need to see (vs 35–43)

The blind beggar leapt at a chance to get help from Jesus. Not even the rebukes of the crowd stopped him from shouting until he got Jesus' attention. But when he finally stood before Jesus, Jesus asked him an unexpected question: 'What do you want me to do for you?' (v 41) In one sense, his need was obvious, since the man was blind; but Jesus didn't assume that the blind man wanted to receive his sight. He desired to hear the man speak out his request. Each time we approach God in prayer, he already knows our needs though it helps us to make them verbal. As expected, when the man asked for his sight, he received what he asked for. What is your prayer and petition to Jesus today?

Prayer: Lord Jesus, who made the blind see, lift the veil from my eyes so I can understand your Word and know you more.

Jesus seeks and saves

You can be saved regardless of your circumstances.

LUKE 19:1–10

Main verse: 'For the Son of Man came to seek and to save what was lost.'

Sought by Jesus (vs 1–6)

Zacchaeus went out seeking Jesus. Perhaps he wasn't fully aware of his deep-seated spiritual needs but simply wanted to see what Jesus was like. People's spiritual quest after God is sometimes sparked by simple curiosity. Nonetheless, God uses that to draw them to himself. His desire to see Jesus was strong enough for him to climb a tree, despite its foolish appearance. As a despised person, Zacchaeus the tax collector was greatly surprised to find Jesus acknowledging him and wanting to spend time with him (v 5). Jesus was seeking him because he came to save those who are spiritually lost. Can you recall the different ways Jesus came seeking you?

Saved by Jesus (vs 7–10)

Encountering Jesus, Zacchaeus became aware of the necessary changes he had to make in his life. Salvation through Jesus brings dramatic changes in lives. Zacchaeus' life was radically transformed. He repented his sins and showed the fruit of repentance in his life. He promised to make a restitution to people whom he had cheated in the past (v 8). Heavenly rewards outweigh any earthly sacrifice we make. Zacchaeus received salvation that day and received forgiveness for his sins. Jesus declared him to be a son of Abraham (v 9). This person who had been rejected and despised by people became fully accepted into God's family. He who had been lost in sin was found by God. What are the fruits of repentance in your life?

Prayer: Lord, all heaven's glory was yours, but you left it to rescue a wretch like me. How can I ever thank you enough?

Fulfil your responsibilities

Jesus expects you to use your gifts for him.

LUKE 19:11–27

Main verse: 'He replied, "I tell you that to everyone who has, more will be given, but as for the one who has nothing, even what he has will be taken away."'

Jesus gives responsibility (vs 11–19)

Though God needs no assistance, he chose from the beginning to use men and women to do his work in the world. God does not expect everyone to accomplish the same things. He gives different gifts and abilities to people so that we would be responsible and use wisely what he has blessed us with. God desires faithfulness from his people, and rewards work well done in his service. He also entrusts greater tasks to those who have been consistently faithful in the small things (v 26). What special gifts have you received from God? In what ways are you using them for his glory?

Jesus judges irresponsibility (vs 20–27)

One servant in this story did nothing with the money he received from his master (v 20). This servant's laziness kept him from taking on his responsibility with the money entrusted to him. He made his excuses by blaming the master for being such a hard man (v 21). Irresponsibility will be judged by God. The man lost his gift and the opportunity to be part of his master's work. What responsibility have you received from God? Are you fulfilling it and taking part in the Master's work?

Prayer: Help me, my Master, to use the gifts you've given me, and to earn your commendation, 'Well done, my good servant'.

King of peace

Jesus came to bring us peace – praise him!

LUKE 19:28–40

Main verse: 'Blessed is the king who comes in the name of the Lord! Peace in heaven and glory in the highest!'

Give willingly (vs 28–35)
It was time to reveal Jesus' identity as the King of kings. Through one action, he wanted to dispel the wrong ideas of what his kingship meant. Therefore we see the King of kings humbly sending two disciples to borrow a colt (vs 30,31). Though perplexed, they obeyed his command. The colt's owners graciously accepted Jesus' request, and because they did, many people saw Jesus as the King of peace. A king who rides on a colt brings peace, not war. Jesus came to bring peace – with God, with others and with ourselves. Do you have a willing and obedient heart toward Jesus today? How will you bless the King of peace today?

Praise enthusiastically (vs 36–40)
There were two different reactions to Jesus as the King of peace. First, there was praise (vs 37,38). Many people showed their enthusiasm by word and deed. They threw their cloaks before his entrance (v 36). Our actions can often exhibit enthusiasm more than words can. However we express it, we should praise God enthusiastically for all he has done for us. The second reaction to Jesus was unbelief. Some people may have felt that Jesus was not worthy to be praised and withheld their praise. Yet regardless of such reaction, the praises of God came forth. Praise and lift up the name of Jesus with all your heart.

Prayer: I bless you Jesus, for you are King, and by your coming I have discovered peace with the God who made me.

Jesus wept

Jesus weeps whenever he finds hypocrisy in his people.

LUKE 19:41–48

Main verse: 'As he approached Jerusalem and saw the city, he wept over it.'

Jesus prophesies judgement (vs 41–44)

Approaching Jerusalem, Jesus wept. He wept because it was a city which had missed its opportunity. Had the people accepted and submitted to Jesus, peace with God would have been established. But now it was too late, and they had missed their chance (v 42). They became blind to the truth. Also, Jesus wept over Jerusalem because of its coming judgement. It would soon fall under the rule of Roman government and be left in ruins. The inevitable consequence of rejecting Jesus Christ is judgement and destruction. When Jesus comes close to your life, what does he find? Does he weep over your missed opportunities?

Jesus exposes hypocrisy (vs 45–48)

In Jerusalem, Jesus went to the temple to expose the hypocrisy of the leaders of God's people. God's house was meant to be a place of communion, but instead it had been turned into a place where the love of money had taken precedence over everything else (v 46). When Jesus comes close to our lives, he exposes many forms of hypocrisy. We are faced with a choice every time we approach the Word of God. We can either reject Jesus or we can receive his Word which helps purge us of any hypocrisy. What is your response when Jesus reveals sin in your life? Why not pray for Jesus to reveal your true heart now?

Prayer: Father, hypocrisy lurks in my heart. Turn your searchlight on me, expose my darkness and help me to turn from it.

Jesus – a man of authority

Jesus is silent to those who will not submit to him.

Main verse: 'Jesus said, "Neither will I tell you by what authority I am doing these things."'

A question of authority (vs 1–4)

Jesus taught the Word of God with relevance and authority, unlike any other leader. Jesus performed miracles, healed the sick and cast out demons with absolute authority. Naturally the leaders were jealous, and decided to question Jesus about his authority (v 2). In response, Jesus posed a question concerning the authority of John the Baptist (vs 3,4). Jesus was well aware of the fact that these people had a problem with authority. They were unwilling to accept or submit to anyone else's authority, and Jesus wanted to expose this inherent arrogance. Do you find it difficult submitting to God's authority in your life? How can you pray about this?

A question of submission (vs 5–8)

Jesus' piercing question exposed two basic problems these people had. First, it exposed their problem with submission – specifically to God. By admitting John the Baptist's divine authority, they would have to submit to it (v 5). That was the last thing they wanted to do. Secondly, it exposed their fear of man, not of God. They were afraid to negate John's authority because many people believed in him (v 6). When we submit to the authority of God in our lives, we are set free from fears. When we refuse to submit fully to God's authority, our lives are bound to the shackles of this world. Are there fears you need to be freed of? How can you submit yourself to the Lord today?

Prayer: Spirit of the living God, fall afresh on me; break me, melt me, mould me, fill me; that I may make Jesus truly Lord.

Are you part of God's plan?

God's plans will never be defeated.

LUKE 20:9-18

Main verse: 'Jesus looked directly at them and asked, "Then what is the meaning of that which is written: 'The stone the builders rejected has become the capstone'?"'

Don't reject the Word (vs 9–12)

This parable illustrates the history of the Jewish people, but it contains challenges for us today. Just as the man planted a vineyard and rented it out to some farmers, so the Lord has planted his Word in our hearts. He has planted the seed of faith and expects to reap fruit from our lives. But when the owner sent the servants to receive the expected fruit, the farmers rebelled by beating the servants and sending them away empty-handed (vs 10-12). The Jewish people often rejected God's message sent through his prophets. God was very patient by sending prophet after prophet, but they continually rejected his Word. Have you rejected some words God has been speaking to you recently?

Don't reject Jesus (vs 13–18)

In view of the constant rejection of his message by the Jewish people, God made one last attempt to reach them. Like the owner in the story, God decided to send his own Son, trusting that they would receive and respect him (v 13). But instead of receiving Jesus, people killed him, hoping to be free from the One they had to submit to. Nevertheless, God turned their rebellion around to fulfil his plan. God's will cannot be thwarted. When the Jewish people rejected Jesus, God found a new people for himself among the Gentiles. Furthermore, through the Jewish people's rejection of his Son, God raised him to the highest position of all. Have you chosen Jesus? Does it encourage you to know that you are part of his plan?

Prayer: Father, thank you that neither indifference nor resistance, either in me or in others, can ever defeat your plans.

Submit to God and the government

Paying taxes is part of your responsibility before God.

LUKE 20:19–26

Main verse: 'He said to them, "Then give to Caesar what is Caesar's, and to God what is God's."'

Submit to God (vs 19–22)

The parable of the tenants came to be fulfilled as the Jewish leaders rejected God's Word and schemed to trap, arrest and kill Jesus. By raising the issue of paying taxes to Rome, they felt they had found the perfect means to convict Jesus. If Jesus told them not to pay taxes, then they could report him as a revolutionist to the government; but if he told them that they must pay their taxes, he would lose popularity with the people. Their flattering words were all true. Jesus taught what was right and without partiality, but sadly they still refused to accept him. In their heart of hearts, they knew that Jesus had the truth. They simply refused to submit. Is your heart submitted to him?

Submit to the government (vs 23–26)

Jesus was uncompromising in his answer. He was not afraid of the leaders. Nor was he afraid of the people. His concern was not over the loss of popularity; his first commitment was to God and to his truth. As far as Jesus was concerned, government should be honoured and obeyed in so far as its demands do not conflict with God's will. Romans 13 teaches that governments receive their authority from God whereby financial support is necessary to govern the society. Christians are obligated to pay taxes. Deceit or flattery will not escape God's notice. Are you faithful and honest in giving to the government what you owe? How about to God?

Prayer: Lord, paying taxes and Sunday offerings seem so different, but you connect them. Help me to give both ungrudgingly.

Is there a resurrection?

Are you looking forward to being with God for ever?

Luke 20:27–40

Main verse: 'He is not the God of the dead, but of the living, for to him all are alive.'

Jesus believes in resurrection (vs 27–36)

The Sadducees had no real intention of submitting to Jesus. In fact, the Sadducees did not believe God's Word or in the resurrection. And in order to mock such teaching, they came up with the example of the widow who married seven brothers. Jesus was uncompromising in his answer to them. First, he expressed very firmly his own belief in the resurrection of the dead (v 35). Those who are found to be worthy by their faith in Jesus will certainly be raised from the dead to enjoy eternal life. But second, Jesus seized the opportunity to teach about eternal life (vs 35,36). Clearly it will not be the same as life on earth. In heaven, the emphasis will be on our relationship with God himself more than with other people. Are you developing your relationship with God now?

Jesus believes in eternal life (vs 37–40)

In order to answer the question the Sadducees had raised, Jesus not only answered with his own words, but also with a clear argument from the Word of God. When Moses described God as the God of Abraham, Isaac and Jacob, he was, in fact, stating his belief that God was the God of the living, not the dead. Jesus confirmed the reality of eternal life and that it would be the reward of all those who believed in God. Those who believe in God now, through the Lord Jesus, will most certainly be rewarded with eternal life. Are you assured of eternal life because you trust Jesus as the living Lord of your life?

Prayer: Lord, you are the Christ, the Son of God and I rejoice that I will share your resurrection life!

Jesus is Lord

Jesus can see straight into our hearts.

LUKE 20:41 – 21:4

Main verses: 'David himself declares in the book of Psalms: "The Lord said to my Lord: 'Sit at my right hand until I make your enemies a footstool for your feet'."'

Jesus is God (vs 41–44)

The Jews revered and honoured David as a great king. They knew the Messiah would be David's descendant. Jesus wanted to open up the minds of those who misunderstood who the Messiah was to be and to open their eyes to see who Jesus was. The Messiah would not be an ordinary man. David understood that the Messiah would be someone infinitely greater than himself to whom he must submit (vs 42–44). He also realised that the Messiah was the Son of God, who would accomplish permanent victory over all his enemies. David did not hesitate to call him 'Lord'. Is Jesus Lord of your life? Do you enjoy all the victory that Jesus has won for you?

Jesus seeks men's hearts (20:45 – 21:4)

For the teachers, outward things were of primary importance. They prided themselves in wearing long clothings of authority. They enjoyed being greeted with distinction. They delighted in taking the best seats at banquets (v 46). They relished making long prayers to impress people, while cheating and deceiving the weak. God is not impressed with outward pretension. God sees right through the hearts of people. The widow had little to show outwardly. She hardly had any material possession to offer to God, but in her heart she gave everything. When Jesus looks at your life, what does he see? Does he see a life engrossed with outward things? Or does he find a heart that is sincerely given to him?

Prayer: Father, I devote so much energy to external things. Help me instead to value a pure and true heart most of all.

Expect persecution

Jesus is with you in the midst of persecution.

LUKE 21:5-19

Main verse: 'All men will hate you because of me.'

Be prepared (vs 5–11)

Jesus predicted the total destruction of the temple (v 6). Jesus' subsequent prediction of the destruction of Jerusalem foreshadows greater destruction of the world on the last day. The events before the destruction of Jerusalem also mirror more terrifying events which will occur before the last day (vs 10,11). There will arise false messiahs (v 8). We must remain alert, for false teachers will lure many into deception. Also, there will be increasing disintegration of our natural world by wars. With these in mind, we can prepare for that day by focusing on eternal things rather than temporal. Where is your heart?

Don't be afraid (vs 12–19)

Preceding both these events would be the persecution of God's people (v 12). Those who have decided to follow Jesus must expect persecution. For some it may be political persecution – being imprisoned, beaten or even killed for Jesus' sake. For others it may mean the cost of family persecution, of being betrayed by those who had loved them (v 16). However, Jesus has assuring promises for those who face persecution. First, he reminds them that all persecution is ultimately aimed at him – 'all on account of my name' (v 12). Second, he promises them that he will be with them and help them know what they should say when the time comes (vs 14,15). Finally, he tells them that even if they must die for him, they will emerge unharmed, for no one can touch their soul (vs 18,19). Are you willing to suffer for Jesus?

Prayer: Lord, talk of suffering scares me. Give me strength and courage to stand for you, whatever the cost may be.

Jesus is coming again!

The end of some things, the beginning of others.

LUKE 21:20–36

Main verse: 'When these things begin to take place, stand up and lift up your heads, because your redemption is drawing near.'

The destruction of Jerusalem (vs 20–24)

Jesus prophesied the destruction of Jerusalem, the primary sign of God's judgement on the Jewish people for the rejection of his Son (vs 20,22). This judgement would usher in a period of God's special grace on the Gentiles. Since the Jews had rejected the gospel, thus forsaking the right to be the people of God, God chose to find his new people among the Gentiles. The judgement brings terrifying consequences as warned by Jesus. There is, however, one ray of hope for the Jews. Verse 24 says that the time of the Gentiles will be fulfilled which implies the same hope expressed in Romans 11 – that God will give the Jewish people one last chance before the end.

The destruction of the world (vs 25–36)

Just as Jerusalem would be destroyed, so too will the world come under God's judgement. Before Jesus returns, certain signs will indicate his coming. Natural chaos is one of the signs of the coming of Jesus. Other signs include increasing political problems, world unrest and a fearful condition among people (vs 25,26). Increasingly, people will give themselves over to a frenzy of pleasure and self-indulgence (v 34). Jesus warns us to be alert and to pray in order to escape the coming judgement (v 36). He exhorts his people to be filled with expectation because, for us, the coming of Jesus will not be the end, but the beginning of a new blessed life. Are you watching and praying? Do you view Jesus' coming as the beginning of a new and blessed life?

Prayer: Lord Jesus, thank you that you are coming in power and glory. Help me always to be prepared and ready for you.

A last Passover feast

Take every opportunity God gives you - it may be your last.

Luke 21:37 - 22:13

Main verse: 'Now the Feast of Unleavened Bread, called the Passover, was approaching.'

A last chance to listen (21:37 – 22:6)

Being aware that his death was near, Jesus focused his energy on teaching people (v 37). The people could not get enough of his teaching. Their thirst for God's Word is a challenge to us. How enthusiastically do we seize opportunities to hear the Word of God? Unlike the attentive followers, there were also those who were eager to get rid of Jesus (v 2). Among them was Judas, who had previously been blessed by Jesus, but who now allowed Satan to control his life (vs 3,4). To avoid this deadly predicament, we must keep our hearts open to the Word of God. A heart that thirsts after God's Word can resist the temptations of Satan. Evil influences abounded in Jesus' last days of ministry on earth, but under God's sovereignty they were used to fulfil his purposes. How thirsty are you for God's Word?

A last chance to obey (22:7–13)

Jesus' last Passover celebration embodied great meaning. This Passover feast was meaningful not only because it fulfilled the law of God but also because it would be the last Feast of the Passover celebrated with the disciples. Jesus would soon offer himself up as the Passover Lamb. The freedom from the enemy and from death that the previous Passover lamb won for God's people in Egypt would now be wonderfully fulfilled in Jesus, who would win complete freedom for his people from death forever (Exodus 12:1-30). What a privilege for the disciples and the owner of the house to be involved in such an event. Our obedience in seemingly small events often has everlasting repercussions. Don't minimise your obedience in anything. How can you maximise your obedience to Jesus today?

Prayer: Father, help me to see the little things that come my way today as opportunities to serve you and bring you glory.

The Last Supper

Always remember that Jesus died for you.

LUKE 22:14–23

Main verse: 'And he took bread, gave thanks and broke it, and gave it to them, saying, "This is my body given for you; do this in remembrance of me."'

The body of Christ (vs 14–19)

This was the last time Jesus would celebrate the Passover with his disciples. The Passover Feast would finally be fulfilled in the death of Jesus. Jesus knew exactly what was to happen to him on the cross. He knew he would have to suffer like the lamb during the first Passover. He knew he had to be slain for his people. Nothing short of the body of Christ offered on the cross would be sufficient to deal with the problems of sin and death faced by the people of God. Jesus could face the prospect of such a death with thanksgiving in his heart (vs 17,19). Every time we partake of the bread broken for us in a communion service, we remember that Jesus died for us. Do you remember to give thanks to Jesus for taking your sins away?

The blood of Christ (vs 20–23)

No sacrifice for sin is acceptable unless blood, the symbol of life, is shed in the place of the sinner who deserves death. The cup of communion is a constant reminder of the blood of Christ shed for us (v 20). At the first Passover, a lamb's blood was smeared on the doorposts. Only when the angel of death saw the blood did he pass over the house and not bring death to that home. Likewise today, only those who believe in the shed blood of Christ will be passed over by God on the day of judgement and not be cast into eternal condemnation. Sadly, there will be those like Judas who, having received many blessings from God, refuse to submit themselves to the Saviour. Are you fully trusting in the blood of Christ for your salvation?

Prayer: Wine and bread: so simple, so significant. Help me not to miss any opportunity to remember your sacrifice for me.

Who is the greatest?

To be the greatest, you need to be a servant.

LUKE 22:24–38

Main verse: 'For who is greater, the one who is at the table or the one who serves? Is it not the one who is at the table? But I am among you as one who serves.'

Serve the Lord (vs 24–30)
Despite the most heart-rending revelation of Jesus' imminent death, the disciples were preoccupied with who would have the highest position in the kingdom of God. Jesus had just shared about the greatest self-sacrifice in human history, and yet the disciples only thought about themselves. Despite their selfish squabbling, Jesus graciously affirmed their importance in God's kingdom. To Jesus, the way to greatness is very different from the world's way. True greatness consists in service (vs 26,27). The way to greatness is through the way of humility. If you want to be great in the kingdom of God, learn to serve him and others. In what specific ways are you serving God? How can you become a more humble servant?

Be prepared (vs 31–38)
Jesus gives advice to prepare his disciples of coming events. He reminds them, especially Peter, of the enemy who will do everything possible to undermine the work of God's people (v 31). Faced with such an enemy, we need to remember that Jesus is praying for us (v 32). Being arrogant and boastful, Peter underestimated the enemy. Thus, when we are unguarded, greater possibility exists for falling into temptation. Recognise the enemy, and then trust God completely for power and strength. Jesus fully equips us to successfully carry out God's work. Are you prepared? Are you trusting him for everything you need?

Prayer: Lord Jesus, often I'm so full of myself, as Peter was. Help me, instead, to be humble and dependent on you.

Jesus overcomes temptation

God will always help you in the face of temptation.

LUKE 22:39-53

Main verse: 'Father, if you are willing, take this cup from me; yet not my will, but yours be done.'

Jesus submits to God's will (vs 39–46)

It was not easy for Jesus to submit to his Father's will. He was about to face the greatest temptation of his life. He would be tempted to turn from doing the will of the Father. When we are faced with temptation there are several truths we can learn from Jesus. First, the best way to overcome temptation is to take it to God in prayer. Prayer keeps us from falling into temptation (vs 40,46). Second, call on the support of others in prayer. Third, regardless of how strong the temptation may be, we must affirm our faith in the will of God for us. God knows exactly what is best. Finally, we need to realise God's constant presence with us, knowing he is ready to help in the midst of temptation. What temptations plague you these days? How do you overcome your temptations?

Jesus overrules the powers of darkness (vs 47–53)

In submitting to his Father's will, Jesus allowed the power of darkness to take place for a time. It began with the betrayal by Judas. However, Jesus refused to give in to violence and hypocrisy. Instead, he demonstrated superiority over the powers of evil and established himself as the Prince of Peace. Jesus' method was peace, as portrayed in healing the servant. Peter's action lacked self-control, using violence to counter the other's violence. Jesus also exposed the hypocrisy of those who intended to arrest him (vs 52,53). Through God's help, we must resist wickedness and defend our lives from the power of evil. How do you confront evil's power? Have you made Jesus your defender in this battle?

Prayer: Lord Jesus, help me to be vigilant and prayerful, so that I do not fall into temptation today.

Don't deny Jesus

As you draw near to God, greater temptations seek to hinder your progress.

LUKE 22:54–62

Main verse: 'The Lord turned and looked straight at Peter. Then Peter remembered the word the Lord had spoken to him. "Before the cock crows today, you will disown me three times."'

Be ready for temptation (vs 54–60)

Before we condemn Peter for his denial of Jesus, we should remember his concern for the Lord. He did not run away and abandon Jesus as the other disciples had. He tried to support Jesus in his hour of need. Had he fled like the other disciples, he could have avoided people's suspicion, but he risked remaining by Jesus. Hence, before pointing out other people's failures, we might ask ourselves whether our distance from Jesus keep us from realising our own failures – that we weren't allowing ourselves to be challenged for his sake. Here, Peter's independence and self-confidence had to be exposed in order to be a suitable servant of Jesus. Where do you place your confidence? In Christ, or in your own strength and ability?

Be ready to repent (vs 61,62)

The moment the cock crowed, Peter realised his failure, and Jesus looked at him. His look expressed neither rebuke nor contempt. Rather, Jesus conveyed tenderness, his understanding look offered Peter forgiveness. Nevertheless Peter, weeping bitterly, could think of nothing else but his sin. When broken over sin, we also must humbly bring ourselves to repent before God for the sins we have committed. Regardless of how deeply we fall into sin or how publicly we have denied Jesus, his forgiveness will restore and reconcile us to him if we repent. Have you been broken over particular sins in your life recently? How have you expressed your repentance?

Prayer: Father, when I'm broken by my sin, lift my eyes to the cross and open my ears to hear your word of pardon.

Who is Jesus?

Jesus openly admitted his identity as the Son of God.

LUKE 22:63–71

Main verse: 'They all asked, "Are you then the Son of God?"
He replied, "You are right in saying I am."'

Is Jesus the Christ?
(vs 63–69)

The guards eagerly mocked and insulted Jesus. The rejection he received was a necessary part of his identification with our sin which he willingly dealt with. No insult could deny Jesus as the Messiah sent by God. Jesus realised that proclaiming himself as the Christ would not necessarily change their hearts, which were already hardened. Nevertheless, Jesus confessed himself as the Son of Man destined to sit at God's right hand. The men who heard this confession would have no excuse on the day of judgement. They needed to know precisely whom they were rejecting. Are you willing to be insulted in order to identify with Jesus?

Is Jesus the Son of God?
(vs 70,71)

The Jews asked Jesus the ultimate question: 'Are you the Son of God?' When Jesus answered that he was, he was resigning himself for arrest and even death, because such an admission was considered blasphemy. To the Jews, there was no other God but Yahweh alone. But their minds were closed to the teaching of their own scriptures. Certainly, if Jesus wasn't truly the Son of God he would not have admitted it. A simple denial of his true identity would have brought the whole matter to an end and Jesus would have been set free. But to remain faithful to who he was, an acknowledgment was made at the risk of his life. Their unbelief neglected and opposed this truth, but we must acknowledge and embrace the truth, accepting Jesus for exactly who he is. Are you prepared to acknowledge Jesus at any cost – even at the risk of your life?

Prayer: Lord Jesus, I believe you are the Christ, the Son of God. Make me bold, so that I never try to hide my faith in you.

King of the Jews

Jesus was innocent of all wrongful accusations.

LUKE 23:1–12

Main verse: 'So Pilate asked Jesus, "Are you the king of the Jews?" "Yes, it is as you say," Jesus replied.'

Jesus and Pilate (vs 1–7)

Jewish leaders were determined to get rid of Jesus. They accused him of two crimes that Pilate, the Roman governor, had to contend with. The first concerned paying taxes to Rome and the second concerned Jesus' claim to be the king. But even Pilate determined that Jesus posed no threat to Rome. Pilate declared him innocent (v 4). In fact, Jesus was innocent not only of those crimes, but of any sin. Because of his sinlessness, he could die in our place. Yet Pilate opted to pass the final decision on to another person, Herod. Pilate desired relief from the complications of this trial. The issue of deciding Jesus' destiny was a difficult matter. Do you tend to avoid conflicts by passing on your responsibilities to others?

Jesus and Herod (vs 8–12)

Herod's curiosity about Jesus mainly concerned Jesus' supernatural power to perform miracles. His interest was not in the spiritual truths Jesus taught. Knowing this may have prevented Jesus from answering Herod's questions (v 9). Those who approach the gospel with wrong motives will find it difficult to believe the good news. The true state of Herod's heart was soon revealed when he mocked Jesus and sent him back to Pilate (v 11). Interestingly, we learn of the friendship that developed between Pilate and Herod because of this experience. Love for Jesus has a uniting effect, but opposition against him also draws people together. Both men were to play pivotal roles in determining the fate of Jesus. With what motives do you approach Jesus?

Prayer: 'Bearing shame and scoffing rude, in my place condemned he stood. Alleluia! What a Saviour!' (Philip Bliss).

Jesus – innocent but condemned

Jesus was exchanged for a murderer. He was also exchanged for you.

LUKE 23:13–25

Main verse: 'He released the man who had been thrown into prison for insurrection and murder, the one they asked for, and surrendered Jesus to their will.'

Crucify him, crucify him! (vs 13–20)

Jesus was innocent from their accusations of political crime or blasphemy. He was sinless. Three times in this passage Pilate asserts the innocence of Jesus (vs 14,20,22). Despite his beliefs regarding Jesus' innocence, however, Pilate failed to follow his conscience and release Jesus. He feared the people and wanted to please them. His fears distorted his sense of justice; his fears forced him to compromise (vs 23,24). Fear has detrimental effects in our lives. The only fear that is right for us to have is the fear of God. The crowd would not compromise, and cried out for Jesus to be crucified. They chose a murderer over a Saviour. Have you made your choice? What things might hinder your sense of justice?

Barabbas, Barabbas! (vs 21–25)

Despite Pilate's pleas on behalf of Jesus, the Jews wanted Barabbas released instead of Jesus. They favoured Barabbas, who had already been convicted and condemned for terrible crimes, over Jesus, who was innocent. They demanded Jesus' death. This trial illustrates the essence of the gospel – the purpose of Jesus' life was to die in the place of sinners. Barabbas, who deserved death, could receive his freedom through the death of Jesus Christ. Since that time, men and women throughout the world have found the same freedom through Jesus Christ. Everyone deserves death, because all have sinned. But freedom from judgement and death is possible through Jesus Christ. Have you come to enjoy that freedom?

Prayer: 'Guilty, vile and helpless we; spotless lamb of God was he: Alleluia! What a Saviour!' (Philip Bliss).

Father, forgive them!

Instead of judgement, Jesus offered forgiveness to the guilty people.

LUKE 23:26-38

Main verse: 'Jesus said, "Father, forgive them, for they do not know what they are doing." And they divided up his clothes by casting lots.'

The cross of judgement (vs 26-31)

The crucifixion of Jesus meant different things to people. Involuntarily, Simon from Cyrene got involved in a personal way in the process of carrying out the death of Christ. He took part in Jesus' suffering on the way to the cross and yet he was able to help Jesus at his weakest. The faithful people who followed him supported Jesus with their presence and expressed their sorrow in tears. Jesus' death posed one final warning of judgement upon those who reject the Lord. The cross of Jesus Christ remains the symbol of salvation to those who believe, but a symbol of judgement to all who reject him. To which group do you belong? What does the cross of Jesus mean in your life today?

The cross of forgiveness (vs 32-38)

Two criminals were crucified with Jesus. He was made to look like a criminal for us. He completely identified himself with sinners. Soldiers, at the foot of his cross, were oblivious to his pain and his words, instead mocking Jesus by gambling for who should get his clothes. Those who had once followed him now mocked him. The sign above Jesus' head ironically revealed who he was, yet no one believed. Facing ridicule, rejection and indifference, he offered words of forgiveness. That was what his death was all about – to forgive people's sins. Can you forgive those who mock and reject you? Is there any sin that Jesus cannot forgive?

Prayer: Lord, this day you plumbed the depths of pain; yet you forgave those doing it to you. Help me to follow your example.

Saved at the cross

Even as he was dying, Jesus offered salvation.

LUKE 23:39–49

Main verse: 'Jesus answered him, "I tell you the truth, today you will be with me in paradise."'

A criminal – saved by grace (vs 39–43)

There were different reactions to Jesus' crucifixion. One of the criminals insulted Jesus as one who couldn't even save himself, let alone anyone else (v 39). The other, however, thought differently. He listened to Jesus' words on the cross. Not only did he acknowledge Jesus' innocence, but faced with imminent death, in his guilt, he committed himself to Jesus (v 42). His act of trust was all that was necessary – then, and now. Essentially, Jesus demands from us an acknowledgement of our sin and a willingness to trust in him. During those last minutes, the repentant criminal received the promise of salvation (v 43). Does this man's example help you to simply trust Jesus despite your circumstances?

A centurion – saved by grace (vs 44–49)

Jesus' sacrificial death affects everyone – Jews as well as Gentiles. The centurion at Golgotha was a Gentile who also recognised Jesus as a righteous man. He opened his heart and praised God. The burden of sin laid on Jesus was symbolised by darkness which fell for three hours. Yet death did not overcome him. He willingly gave himself for us. Through his death, the way into the very presence of God was opened. Anyone can approach God directly in prayer. Will you take advantage of this privilege today? Will you pray for someone who needs to know of God's saving grace today?

Prayer: Lord Jesus, remember me when you come into your kingdom.

Jesus' death was real

Jesus died for you.

Luke 23:50-56

Main verse: 'The women who had come with Jesus from Galilee followed Joseph and saw the tomb and how his body was laid in it.'

Stand out for Jesus (vs 50–54)

Not all the Jewish rulers were against Jesus. Joseph of Arimathea was a man who had been a secret follower of Jesus. He had refused to join with the other rulers in condemning Jesus (v 51). He had probably refused to join with the group but had not actively condemned them either. Opposing the majority requires risk, especially when you occupy a prestigious position. But at the foot of the cross, Joseph made clear his dedication to Jesus. He courageously asked for the body of Jesus for burial. What fears keep you from identifying with Jesus? Let go of those fears today, knowing that ultimately God will acknowledge you as you confess him.

Listen to what Jesus says (vs 55,56)

There was also a group of women who witnessed the death of Jesus. They saw his body laid in the tomb (v 55). They knew exactly where his body had been laid, which means that these women could not have gone to the wrong tomb on the third day since the burial. They were faithful to prepare the body of Jesus. But had they remembered the teaching of Jesus, their preparations would have been unnecessary. Again, we are challenged to trust in his promises. Are you forgetting God's promises? Have you been jumping ahead of God?

Prayer: Father, when I'm embarrassed to admit I'm your child, give me courage to stand up and be counted for who I am.

Jesus conquered death

Jesus is alive today and for evermore.

LUKE 24:1-12

Main verse: 'He is not here; he has risen! Remember how he told you, while he was still with you in Galilee'.

Jesus is alive (vs 1-8)

As soon as the Sabbath was over, the women went to prepare the body of Jesus. But to their surprise they found the tomb open and empty. Then the angels appeared to these women and announced the shattering news of the resurrection. Thus God's Word was fulfilled as foretold (vs 6,7). Indeed, Jesus died but was alive in three days! Though the prophecy may have been vague and incomprehensible then, its truth has now become a reality. We, too, are often confounded by the truths of God's Word. Therefore, we must always be dependent on his guidance in understanding messages in the Scriptures. Ask God to open your eyes to see that Jesus is alive. Do you have new life as a result of Jesus' resurrection?

Believe in the living Jesus (vs 9-12)

Although the disciples were previously informed of Jesus' resurrection, they had little faith to believe. The women offered their testimony of what they had seen, but the disciples could not fully comprehend the reality of this event. When Peter witnessed the evidence of the linen, he was astounded in disbelief. Sadly, unbelief robs us of the ability to see spiritually. Only God can remove the scales of unbelief from our eyes. The women acted wisely by immediately proclaiming the good news of Jesus' resurrection. We are also called to share this news with people around us. Are you eagerly and boldly proclaiming the news that Christ has risen?

Prayer: Living Lord, may the truth that you are alive so thrill me today that my life and words declare your resurrection.

Jesus in the Old Testament

Only God's Spirit reveals spiritual matters.

LUKE 24:13–27

Main verse: 'And beginning with Moses and all the prophets, he explained to them what was said in all the scriptures concerning himself.'

Blinded by unbelief (vs 13–24)

The resurrected body of Jesus transcended the limitations of the ordinary human body. However, the disciples' inability to recognise Jesus was not so much due to this change as to their spiritual blindness and unbelief. Despite Jesus' previous teachings and the testimony of the women that very morning, the two disciples were still gripped by unbelief (vs 21–23). Naturally, when Jesus approached them, they did not recognise him immediately. They were confused and troubled. They desperately needed the assuring presence of Jesus to dispel any doubts. How has drawing near to Jesus helped you to dispel doubts? Are your spiritual eyes open to see Jesus?

Slow to believe (vs 25–27)

In order to bring the disciples to faith, Jesus pointed once more to the Word of God (v 27). The death of Jesus was incomprehensible to them despite the prophecies in the scriptures. So Jesus took them on a journey through the scriptures which spoke of his incarnation, death and resurrection. He would have expounded the significance of the Passover Lamb, the sacrifices in Leviticus, the Messianic Psalms and the passages in Isaiah (v 27). Approaching the Old Testament in the light of Jesus helps us understand God's message clearly. When our faith is weak, God's Word strengthens our faith. How regularly do you study the scriptures to gain greater knowledge of Jesus?

Prayer: Create in me, O Lord, a hunger to know you more; and pour your Spirit on me, that I may I understand your Word.

Spread the good news

Share what Jesus has done in your life.

LUKE 24:28-35

Main verse: 'Then their eyes were opened and they recognised him, and he disappeared from their sight.'

Invite Jesus in (vs 28–32)

Jesus doesn't force his presence on anyone. He graciously draws close to us as he did with the two disciples on the way to Emmaus. And he waits for us to invite him into a closer relationship with us. Jesus willingly accepted the invitation to come into their home. Once invited into our lives, Jesus reveals more of himself to us (vs 30,31). Just as Jesus prepared to have supper with them by giving thanks and breaking the bread, their spiritual eyes were opened and they saw Jesus for who he really was (v 31). Likewise, when we participate in the Lord's Supper we can experience Jesus more deeply and closely. And reading Scripture allows him to speak to us. What is he saying to you today?

Tell someone about Jesus (vs 33–35)

Once the two disciples realised who Jesus was, they were anxious to tell the others of their encounter with him. The other disciples already knew about the great news because Jesus had appeared to Peter. Peter needed the personal appearance of Jesus. He had to know that he was forgiven for his earlier denial of Jesus. Jesus deals with each of us differently. He meets us where we are, ready to forgive and accept in our hour of need. One by one the disciples were realising the amazing truth of Jesus' resurrection. It is the good news which should be proclaimed to everyone. Will you pray for an opportunity to tell someone about Jesus today?

Prayer: Father, give me an opportunity today to speak to someone about Jesus; and the courage to take the opportunity.

Jesus calls and equips

When Jesus calls you, he will also equip you.

LUKE 24:36-53

Main verse: 'I am going to send you what my Father has promised; but stay in the city until you have been clothed with power from on high.'

Jesus really is alive (vs 36–43)

Despite the testimony of witnesses who encountered the resurrected Jesus, the disciples remained in scepticism. When Jesus appeared before them, the disciples thought they were seeing a ghost (v 37). Jesus dispelled their doubts in two ways. First, he showed them the holes in his hands, feet and side – signs that he had been crucified (vs 39,40). Then, he asked for fish and ate it (vs 41-43). Indeed his physical body had been raised from the dead, though it was no longer limited by space and time. We need not be afraid of Jesus. He came to bring us peace. He accomplished it on the cross and through his resurrection. Are you doubtful of Jesus' presence in your life?

Jesus gives power (vs 44–53)

Jesus was about to return to his Father in heaven. The disciples would now be Jesus' representatives on earth. But before he returned to heaven, Jesus had to equip them, first by teaching them the scriptures. From now on they would be able to understand God's Word as they had never been able to understand it before (vs 44-47). Then he commissioned them to preach the gospel throughout the world. Next, he promised divine power to help them fulfil their task. Finally, he blessed them with great joy despite his physical absence. Are you equipped with his power? Is your heart filled with divine joy?

Prayer: Fill me again, Lord God, with your Spirit; give me your power, peace and joy that I may serve you well today.

Scripture Union notes

We hope that you have found *Light where we walk* helpful as you have met God regularly in his Word. Now what?

Most Christian bookshops carry a range of publications designed to help you read the Bible regularly and meaningfully, including Scripture Union's own material. You will have seen on the colour pages something of our range of dated Bible reading materials for adults and children. We also produce a variety of undated notes and other books to help Christians walk in the light.

We have taken the opportunity to include here a sample set of notes which appear in the current (April–June 1998) quarter of *Daily Bread*. This series, on Psalms 85–94, was written by Neil Dougall. The editor, Jenny Hyatt, introduced this quarter with the following comment:

'I find it hugely encouraging that, just as we all have our own ups and downs, so did the characters in the Bible. Wherever we are on our personal roller coaster of faith – whether on a high, a low or even temporarily on the level! – God's Word can meet us right at that point, speaking straight into our situation and surprising us afresh with its relevance. May this be your experience too.'

On the final page you will find a form, which you can use to order Scripture Union notes from the SU Bookshop in Glasgow.

> *Jesus answered, 'The Scriptures say:*
> *"No one can live only on food.*
> *People need every word*
> *that God has spoken."'*
> *(Matthew 4:4)*

WAY IN
to Psalms 85–94

Christians have always treasured the Psalms. Part of the reason for this is captured by a remark attributed to Athanasius: 'Most scripture speaks to us, while the Psalms speak for us.' It is as if, in the Psalms, we eavesdrop on God's people as they pray. In this, the Psalms are a little like the Lord's Prayer. They are prayers which we can use word for word as we talk to God, and they also provide patterns for our own prayers.

All of us, from time to time, are dishonest in prayer. We say what we think we *should* say rather than what we are really thinking and feeling. The Psalms most definitely do not do this. Their honesty is breathtaking. We wouldn't dare talk to God as they do. Yet, because they do, they encourage us to be real in prayer.

The psalms we will look at over the next ten days arise out of a wide range of human circumstances. Psalms 87, 92 and 93 are praise psalms, bright and joyous. Most of the others, though, emerge from situations of difficulty and trouble. Many people grapple with the question: What do I do when what I *experience* in life is very different from what I *expected* God to do? Psalms 91 and 94 are confident and trusting; but on the other hand Psalm 89 is full of questions, Psalm 88 begins and ends in darkness and Psalm 85 expresses a longing for revival.

My prayer is that reading these psalms will encourage you to be real and honest with God as you pray.

THU 7 MAY
Heal our land

Watching the news on TV, do you ever despair and cry, 'How long, O Lord, must I call for help, but you do not listen?' (Habakkuk 1:2)?

PSALM 85

The state of church and society in the West today compares badly with that of former generations. We feel hopelessness and despair as we see standards around us slipping ever lower; we face the future with fear and trepidation. A similar tension between the *past* and the *present* drove this writer to prayer. Out of this, hope for the *future* was born.

In the past (vs 1–3), Israel experienced God's favour (perhaps a reference to the return from exile in Babylon). In the present (vs 4–7), there was hardship (perhaps a reference to the setbacks described in Haggai 1:5–11). Feeling the tension between past and present, the psalmist pleads with God for revival. Then, with this off his chest, he stops talking and listens to God (v 8). What two things emerge from this silence (vs 8,9 and vs 10–13)? Like the psalmist, listening to God can give us a greater sense of confidence and a clearer picture of our situation.

Does the state of society fill you with negative feelings? This psalm shows a positive alternative – pray persistently for the church and the world around you, and to wait humbly before God, asking him to show you what he wants you to do. *'I know your reputation, Lord, and I am amazed at what you have done. Please turn from your anger and be merciful; do for us what you did for our ancestors' (Habbakuk 3:2, CEV).*

> *each me your way, O Lord,*
> *and I will walk in your truth;*
> *give me an undivided heart,*
> *that I may fear your name.*

Psalm 86:11

FRI 8 MAY

Discipline in prayer

When we pray, focusing first on God can help us deal with the hurt others cause us. Take a few moments to worship God before reading today's psalm.

PSALM 86

David felt extremely low and isolated (v 1). In his misery he cried to God for help (vs 3–7). Yet the details of his trouble only emerge towards the end, and then very briefly (v 14). Before, what does he focus on (vs 8–10)? Thinking about God's uniqueness leads David to pray about his own weaknesses (v 11) and to praise God (vs 12,13).

When describing his trouble (v 14), David is measured and restrained, avoiding bitterness and hatred. These feelings have not simply been repressed; instead they seem to have been eased. By focusing first on God and then praying about his own weaknesses, David is able to view those who have hurt him differently. What does he ask for them (v 17) and then for himself (v 16)? David is praying not for their destruction, but rather that they would see the error of their ways; and for himself, mercy and strength. The psalm ends on a note of trust and confidence.

Do you find it easy to pray in this way for those who hurt you? Hard it may be, but it's a discipline worth the effort. For by it you can be released from the anger and bitterness which will only poison your life.

Heavenly Father, help me even in the hardest times to praise you and to acknowledge my own failings.

SAT 9 MAY

Jesus shall reign!

What will heaven be like? There will be more people than can be counted, from every ethnic group around (Revelation 7:9). Ask God to help you grasp the reality of this today.

PSALM 87

Why is Jerusalem (Zion) called the 'city of God' (v 3)? In the Old Testament the temple in Jerusalem was the focus for God's meeting with his people. Jerusalem was not just for Israel's benefit, she was to have a universal role. People from the surrounding nations are described as her citizens (v 4), because they have acknowledged God and worship him.

This psalm's fulfilment comes in John's vision of the new Jerusalem to which all people will come (Revelation 21:22-27). More than a place, the new Jerusalem is the community of God's people (vs 5,6). To it come not just the neighbours of God's people but her enemies too. For Egypt (Rahab) and Babylon (v 4) were superpowers constantly threatening Israel, in the way that secularism and pluralism threaten the church today; Philistia was Israel's local enemy, never completely eradicated, like paganism today; and Tyre was a wealthy trading city, to which we can compare materialism today.

Do you believe this will really happen? The Bible teaches clearly that one day every knee will bow before Jesus (Philippians 2:10,11). The worldwide triumph of God's kingdom is assured. Expect this! Pray for it and work for it!
Lord, help me to believe that Jesus is building his church and nothing can overcome it (Matthew 16:18).

SUN 10 MAY

Deepest darkness

Ask God to help you enter into this prayer: 'Why are you downcast, O my soul? Why so disturbed within me? Put your hope in God, for I will yet praise him, my Saviour and my God' (Psalm 43:5).

PSALM 88

When you see no light at the end of the tunnel, you need faith which clings limpet-like onto God. This kind of faith is seen in this, the bleakest of all psalms, containing scarcely a flicker of light. This makes it one of the most important psalms, for experiences like this come to us all.

From beginning to end it is a tale of woe. The psalmist is as good as dead (vs 3-5), overwhelmed by God's anger (v 7) and shunned by friends (v 8). He prays constantly to God (vs 1,9,13), but it makes no difference. God is hidden from him (v 14). This is not new; it has been his life's pattern (v 15). So the psalmist ends feeling even lower than he started, talking of God's anger (v 16) and the utter loneliness he feels (v 18).

Why does the psalmist bother? If God is so set against him and unresponsive to his prayers, why keep on praying? The paradox is that the psalmist calls God his Saviour (v 1) and persists in prayer. Trouble may have been crashing in like waves on the beach (v 7) but he refuses to let go of God. It is as if he says to himself, 'Somehow, someday it will work out. Until then I will hang on to God, and do this by telling him just how awful life is for me.'
Think of a friend experiencing deep darkness. Ask God to give them the tenacity to hold on to him.

MON 11 MAY
Wrestling with God

God's reliability and faithfulness are very important to us. So what do we do if God seems to break his promises?

PSALM 89

When what you experience in life is different from what you expect, a tension, even a crisis, develops. Then it is tempting to abandon your faith or to retreat from reality, refusing to face the facts. Do you fall into either of these traps? This psalm shows a third option – to wrestle with God in prayer about the problem.

Verses 3 and 4 are this psalm's 'text', words spoken long ago by God to King David (2 Samuel 7:8-16). Now God is accused of breaking his promise (v 39). In fact, the whole nation seems to be under God's wrath (vs 38-45). Reflection makes matters worse. What pattern does the psalmist trace (vs 5-18)? Both creation and history speak of God's faithfulness, and God's promise to David was unambiguous (vs 19-37).

This prompts a humble, probing, questioning prayer which refuses either to abandon God or reality. It displays a rigorous honesty and breathtaking courage. For example what solemn truth does the psalmist remind God of in verses 30-34? It is as if he says to God, 'You promised to punish disobedience but never to break the covenant, so how can you explain what's happening?' But even as he challenges God, he knows that only God can help. So he finishes with a plea to him (vs 46-51).

Lord, when your promises seem to fail, give me the courage to pray as Jacob did, 'I will not let you go unless you bless me' (Genesis 32:26).

TUE 12 MAY
O God our help...

Lord, teach me how short my life is so that I may become wise (v 12, GNB).

PSALM 90

How do you view yourself? As lord of the universe and master of your own destiny, or as temporary and insubstantial (vs 5,6)? In this psalm, human life is painted against the backdrop of God's eternal existence (v 2) and set in the context of the fall (v 3; see Genesis 3:19) which has brought us under the sentence of death (vs 7-10).

Why did Moses write (v 12)? He intended not to depress but to encourage right thinking. For human pride is one of the greatest obstacles to God's grace. Only once it is punctured can we turn to him for help. Life may be short, but instead of moaning under God's wrath (v 9) we can live it joyfully under his love (v 14). Instead of chasing what fades (v 6), we can seek God's splendour, doing his work which lasts (vs 16,17).

For God is now, has been, and always will be a refuge and a home for us (v 1). Imagine what life was like for the Israelites when Moses led them through the wilderness of Sinai. Their wanderings and homelessness are a graphic picture of our life on earth. God was for them a dwelling place, as he will be for you if you are willing to abandon your self-reliance and see yourself as God sees you.

'O God, our help in ages past, / Our hope for years to come, / Be Thou our guard while troubles last / And our eternal home' (Isaac Watts).

> *L*ord, you have been our dwelling-place
>   throughout all generations.
> Before the mountains were born
>   or you brought forth the earth and the world,
>   from everlasting to everlasting
>   you are God.
>
> Psalm 90:1,2

WED 13 MAY
Valuable testimony

The experience of other Christians assists us in our walk of faith. Pause to thank God for an occasion when something that another Christian shared with you helped you.

PSALM 91

This psalm begins not with a textbook theory but a word of testimony. In verses 1 and 2 the psalmist describes the safety and security he himself has found in God (notice the words *I* and *my* in verse 2). In verses 3-13 he applies this to other people (notice how often *you* and *yours* is used). He is saying, 'What God has done for me, he can do for you.'

What kinds of dangers does the psalmist describe (vs 5-7)? These threaten and create terror. But the person who trusts God experiences his help and protection, which is warm and living, and solid and unmoving (v 4). God's angels, though unseen, are real and guard us from danger (v 11). The promise of 'no harm' (v 10) does not mean that nothing will go wrong for God's people, rather that nothing will happen without his permission. All will be used for our ultimate good (Romans 8:28).

Who speaks in verses 14-16? The truth of the psalmist's words is confirmed by God himself. He promises that if we set our hearts on him he will help and protect us. Trouble may come our way (v 15) but in it we will discover God's deliverance. So deep security is shown to be the fruit of seeking after and resting in God.

Is there someone you could speak to today, sharing the security you have found in God, so as to encourage them to take refuge in him?

THU 14 MAY
Right rhythm

'Our society teaches us to oscillate between frenzy and collapse. We commute and cocoon. We have lost the rhythm that develops between abiding and fruitfulness' (J Ortberg, *Leadership*, Spring 1994, p82).

PSALM 92

Praise is productive; it glorifies God and nourishes our beings (vs 1-3). But do you have space for praise in your life? In the rush of modern living, praise gets squeezed out. When this is missing, what dangers lie before us (vs 6,7)? What could be sadder than to devote your life to things which seem so important, but turn out not to be?

Knowing this, God established the rhythm of work and rest (Genesis 2:1-3). He created the Sabbath day (Sunday for most Christians) to give us space for rest and worship, so that we can respond to God for who he is (v 8) and what he has done (v 4). This 'Sabbath psalm' describes the benefits of worship. Firstly, it leads to awe and reflection (v 5). Then, it helps us to see beyond what is obvious and immediate, to understand that God's ultimate victory is certain (vs 9-11). Finally, it feeds our faith. What picture is used to describe regular worshippers (vs 12-14)? Reflect on the features of this picture.

The pressure of modern living means that God's rhythm for life is increasingly under threat. What practical things could you do to ensure that next Sunday remains a Sabbath – a day when there is space for worship and rest?

FRI 15 MAY
Full volume!

Lord, may my heart be touched, my mind informed, my will gripped and my spirit thrilled by your word today.

PSALM 93

Some pieces of music have to be played very loud to be appreciated; similarly, you need to read this psalm at full volume. For while its message may be simple, its impact is powerful. It proclaims, amidst the chaos and confusion of life, that God reigns. In almost every verse, key phrases are repeated two or three times. The repetition drives home the message. If your circumstances permit, try reading this psalm out loud now, as loud as you dare. Let yourself be overwhelmed by the truth that God reigns!

Standing by a sea wall as the waves come crashing in is a humbling experience (v 3). The power of the oceans whipped up by a storm is terrifying; the noise deafening. The roar of the pounding waves captures the daily chaos, tragedy and despair of human life, before which we feel helpless.

But God (v 4) is mightier than the mightiest of earthly forces. They cannot shake him or disturb him. His eternal throne was established long before any of this ever existed (v 2). Better still, though the storm cannot shake him, his heart is touched by our needs and cries. For even the hairs on our heads are numbered (Matthew 10:29-31). Incredibly, the unmovable one is moved by puny humans!

Lord, in all the ups and downs of life today, help me to be quite certain that you reign and remain in control.

To him who is able to keep you from falling and to present you before his glorious presence without fault and with great joy — to the only God our Saviour be glory, majesty, power and authority, through Jesus Christ our Lord, before all ages, now and for evermore! Amen.

JUDE 24,25

SAT 16 MAY

Quick-fix faith?

'O for a faith that will not shrink, though pressed by many a foe, that will not tremble on the brink, of poverty or woe' (W H Bathurst).

PSALM 94

God is the judge of all the earth who does what is right (Genesis 18:25). The writer was sure of this (vs 1,2,23); and so should we be, for Scripture teaches it (2 Corinthians 5:10). But what actually happens around us (vs 4–7)? Tyrants gain power, consider themselves out of reach of God's judgement and heap misery on others. No wonder God's people cry, 'How long, Lord?' (v 3).

Yet this psalmist's tone is confident, not despairing. Was this because injustice was an abstract issue for him (vs 16–19)? Not at all. The psalmist has suffered greatly, yet his prayer arises out of a deep-seated conviction that God, the judge, will most definitely do what is right. So he mocks the arrogance of tyrants who think they answer to no one (vs 8–11), he recalls God's unbreakable covenant with Israel (v 14) and he takes shelter under God's wings (v 22).

We envy faith like this. Where did it come from (v 12)? The psalmist had accepted God's discipline and studied his scriptures. This was a faith refined in the fire, not picked up prepacked on the way out of church. It was not an overnight creation, but the product of a life of discipleship. *Will you learn from this psalmist that there is no quick fix of faith? Which of your attitudes towards God's discipline and the Bible do you need to change in order to develop this sort of faith?*

Notes order form

You may order your notes from your local Christian bookshop
or by post from Scripture Union Bookshop, 9 Canal Street, Glasgow G4 0AB.

Bible reading notes	Subscription		Individual	
	Price*	Qty	Price*	Qty
Alive to God (for adults, 3 quarters only)	8.85		2.95	
Daily Bread (for adults)	11.20		2.95	
Large Type Daily Bread	11.20		2.95	
Encounter with God (for adults)	11.20		2.95	
Let's Go (7–9s)	12.90		2.35	
Check it Out! (9–11s) – Binder	6.49			
– Quarterly pages	12.90		3.49	
One Up (11–14s)	10.30		2.70	

Please begin my annual subscription in   Jan ☐   Apr ☐   Jul ☐   Oct ☐

Closer to God (bimonthly for adults)	13.20		2.45	

Please begin my annual subscription in   Jan ☐ Mar ☐ May ☐ Jul ☐ Sep ☐ Nov ☐

Prices valid until September 1998

Total: £_____

Gift to Scripture Union's ministry: £_____

Total amount enclosed: £_____

PAYMENT WITH ORDER IS REQUIRED

Name_____

Address_____

_____ Postcode_____

Tel No (if paying by credit card)_____

I enclose my postal order/cheque** made payable to Scripture Union

Please debit my Access/Mastercard/Switch/Visa** card

Card No ☐☐☐☐ ☐☐☐☐ ☐☐☐☐ ☐☐☐☐

Expiry Date ☐☐☐☐   Switch Issue No ☐☐☐   Date ☐☐☐☐☐

Signature_____

Cardholder Name_____

*prices include p&p   **delete as appropriate   LWWW